TBN Networks: Celebrating 50 Years of God's Faithfulness

TRILOGY

Trilogy Christian Publishers

A Wholly Owned Subsidiary of Trinity Broadcasting Network

2442 Michelle Drive
Tustin, CA 92780

ISBN-13: 979-8-88738-516-7

TABLE OF CONTENTS

NETWORKS

CELEBRATING 50 YEARS OF GOD'S FAITHFULNESS

TBN FOUNDERS PAUL AND JAN CROUCH

"In those early days of TBN, problems too many to count drove us to our knees in prayer. We felt much like Abraham, who obeyed God when told to leave his home. '… he went out, not knowing whither he went' (Hebrews 11:8, KJV). It was in those times of uncertainty that God taught us true faith!" — Paul F. Crouch

Faith is walking to the edge
of all the light you have...
...and taking one more step.

Paul F. Crouch

TBN REMEMBERS

JANICE WENDELL CROUCH
1938-2016

PAUL FRANKLIN CROUCH, SR.
1934-2013

> "...we were unqualified but available, and that's why God used us."
>
> *Paul F. Crouch*

A Legacy of God's Faithfulness / by Paul F. Crouch, Sr.

Paul Crouch wrote the following in 2013 just shortly before his passing, on the occasion of TBN's 40th anniversary.

Over forty years ago God raised up the Trinity Broadcasting Network for His glory and to send His saving grace to all the world! As I ponder these awesome forty years I am compelled to think of Moses and the forty years of wandering through the wilderness with the children of Israel. What were his thoughts as he stood on Mount Nebo overlooking the land of promise? I cannot help but wonder.

I also wonder how close we are to our promised land? On the one hand I could almost feel that we have arrived. TBN is proclaiming the gospel around the world in many languages, through two dozen networks on scores of satellite channels, feeding TV stations, cable systems, and home satellite receivers, as well as reaching the Internet through streaming

(714) 731-1000

and video-on-demand! Who could have dreamed of an iTBN with video-on-demand? Wonder of wonders, through it many of those great souls now in heaven are still preaching and teaching the Word. Yes, even though they are dead, they still speak (Hebrews 11:4).

In one final sense I, too, stand at "Jordan's stormy banks." Will I be blessed even more than Moses who was only permitted to see the Promised Land from afar? Only God knows. But let us agree now — as long as we have life and breath — that together we will cross our stormy Jordan, and we will possess our Jerichos and lands of promise! Yes, we will continue taking territory away from the evil one until that glorious day when we all awaken in our final land of promise. Ah, Beulah Land, sweet Beulah Land!

Dear partners, Jan and I will never meet many of you in this world or lifetime, but I promise you with all my heart that we will have one great TBN rally on that day "JUST INSIDE THE EASTERN GATE OVER THERE"!

We love you. Godspeed, and Maranatha!

P.S. Sing one last song with me:
I won't have to cross Jordan alone,
Jesus died all my sins to atone,
In the darkness I see,
He'll be waiting for me,
I won't have to cross Jordan alone.

Paul F. Crouch

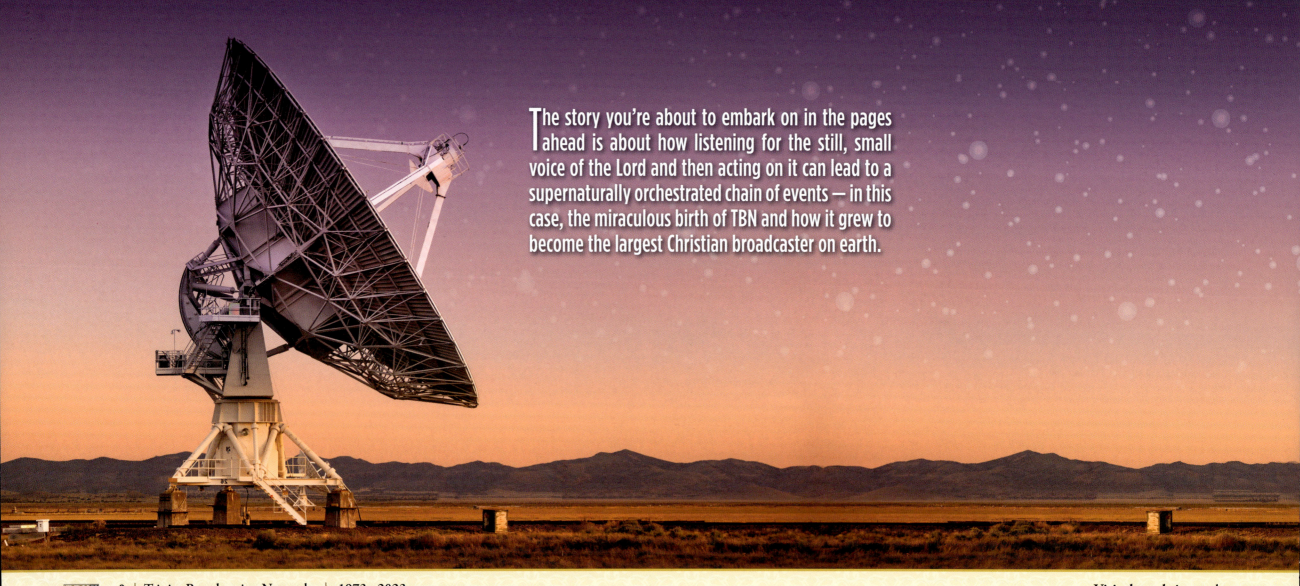

The story you're about to embark on in the pages ahead is about how listening for the still, small voice of the Lord and then acting on it can lead to a supernaturally orchestrated chain of events — in this case, the miraculous birth of TBN and how it grew to become the largest Christian broadcaster on earth.

Following "The Call"

G od is calling—to you, to me, to every person on the face of the earth. His call is one of compassion and mercy, to a "future and a hope," and it begins with forgiveness and salvation. Jesus said: "Behold, I stand at the door and knock. If anyone hears My voice and opens the door, I will come in...."

For those who answer the call and surrender their lives to Him, Jesus promises a lifetime of destiny and purpose. Of course, reaching that purpose will require that we surrender our will and our own wisdom to His, and to trust Him to lead us each step of the way. While that might make many of us who are used to charting our own courses uncomfortable and uncertain, He promises that if we simply turn to Him every moment of every day, looking to Him as our source and guide, He will direct our paths and bring us to our desired end.

God's purpose is unique for each and every person, but it is all tied to

> "For those who answer the call and surrender their lives to Him, Jesus promises a lifetime of destiny and purpose."

one common end—to see His kingdom come and His will done "on earth as it is in heaven." And don't worry, God is not looking for the smartest, the wealthiest, or the most talented people to fulfill His eternal purpose. He is looking for those who are available, who will say "Yes!" to His call. Your flaws and failures don't matter, nor what others say or think. The only opinions that matter are yours and God's—and in His heart and mind, you are a victor.

The story in the pages ahead is about what happened when two people said "Yes" to God's call, and took the path to that unique destiny God had chosen for them, a path that led to the miraculous birth of TBN. Paul and Jan often said that following God's call took them through many challenging and faith-testing circumstances. But it is those challenges and tests that lead to the victory and blessing God promises to those who will follow Him unreservedly.

"... a Future and a Hope"

When Paul and Jan began their journey, they had little idea of the road ahead. They only knew God was calling them to a lifetime of trusting Him, and a destiny only He could fulfill.

The seeds of 100-percent Christian television germinated for Paul in 1971 when he helped build a tiny station launched by Faith Center Church in Glendale, California.

Hello, World: *Paul helped launch the campus radio station at Central Bible College in Springfield, Missouri.*

New Leaders . . . The Rev. Bernard Ridings, pastor and assistant pastor of the Central Ridings and Mrs. Crouch, respectively, from Rapid City. . . . ning activities for their new charge. (Chronicle P

Central Assembl
Pastors Arrive

Midwest boy meets southern belle: *Paul and Jan met at a church camp in South Dakota — love at first sight!*

August 25, 1957 — the happy couple poses in Columbus, Georgia with Jan's parents, Pastor and Mrs. Edgar Bethany (left), along with Paul's mother, Sarah Crouch, and his best man, Bernard Ridings.

In the early 1960s Paul (r) helped pioneer TV and film production for the Assemblies of God.

KHOF NEWS KHOF NEWS

Our staff for KHOF Radio and TV now numbers more than 40 full and part-time employees. Each one loves our Lord and is dedicated to world evangelization. We only wish that all of you, our wonderful KHOF co-partners could appear with us in this picture, as you are just as much a part of this ministry as we. What a large picture that would be!

Thank you for loving, praying and sharing.

PAUL F.

"I Release You..."

It started with a word from the Lord as Paul and Jan Crouch were helping a local Southern California church with its television ministry. "The idea of TV devoted to Christian programming was radical in 1973," recalled Paul, "but the first seeds were planted by our own pastor, who wanted to use television in his church's ministry and turned us loose to get a part-time station on the air."

Things could not have been going better as Paul and Jan arrived at the Hollywood High School auditorium on the evening of March 10, 1973, for a rally to celebrate the miracle of Christian television that was going out a few hours a day through the church's UHF station. Excitement was high as Christians caught the vision of how TV could be used to win the lost and encourage people in their faith. "We felt certain we had found our Promised Land," recalled Jan, "the place where God would use us for the long haul." Little did the

> "God has a destiny for each of us. Hearing His call and stepping out in faith are key to getting there."
> – Paul F. Crouch

Crouches know that God was about to call them to a new place of destiny.

That evening Paul watched as special musical guest Doug Oldham ministered to a packed auditorium. Afterwards hundreds from the crowd lingered to express their support for Christian television.

But as Paul and Jan drove home that night, basking in the contentment that they'd found where they belonged, God spoke a quiet word to Paul that left him speechless: *"I release you from this ministry...."*

"Had I heard the Lord correctly?" Paul recalled wondering. "But when I turned to Jan, she had that knowing look in her eye, and she assured me, 'Yes, I heard it too. God has released you from your work, and He has a new direction for us.'"

New direction came quickly as Paul and Jan sought the Lord, and within two months God provided a little station that was the beginning of Trinity Broadcasting Network.

"**M**ountains high and valleys low — ah yes. But 'if I'd never had a problem, I wouldn't know God could solve them, I'd never know what faith in God could do.' Praise God — He has solved them all! Thanks for the song, dear cousin Andraé Crouch!"

— Paul F. Crouch

Site for
Trinity Broadcasting Network
(714) 731-1000

As Paul and Jan discovered, following God's call requires faith. Scripture offers us the clear example of Abraham, who *"obeyed when he was called to go out to the place which he would receive as an inheritance. And he went out, not knowing where he was going"* (Hebrews 11:8, NKJV).

"...work was non-stop, and you rested when— and where—you could." – Jan

What an honor to bring people's needs before the Lord, knowing He is the answer.

On the Praise the Lord *set with dear friend T.L. Osborn.*

Faithful friends and ministry partners in prayer.

The prayer and support of Christian leaders like Pastor Jerry Barnard were a blessing to Paul and Jan as they worked to guide TBN.

TBN's first studio was a rented office building at 111 W. Dyer Road in Santa Ana, California.

"When TBN launched on May 28, 1973, we had to hit the ground running, and that meant creating new programs to fill the time we were on the air each day. From *Praise the Lord* and *Behind the Scenes* to kids' and women's programs, music shows, and Bible studies, God blessed our efforts with His anointing. And in the years ahead our production got a whole lot better! — Jan Crouch"

Paul Crouch (right) hosted an early TBN Praise *program, while prayer partners manned the phones to pray with viewers who called in with needs.*

Paul, Jan (with broom), and a core of committed volunteers worked nearly round-the-clock to transform TBN's first studio.

Jan (second from right) hosted an early TBN program for women titled Happiness Is.

Early control room in TBN's first studio.

> "Jan's precious father, Edgar 'Papa' Bethany, lived to see TBN receive its first TV station, KTBN Channel 40 in Southern California. Sadly, he left us in 1975, but taped four classic Bible study programs: *Jesus Savior, Healer, Baptizer in the Holy Spirit,* and *Coming King!* To me there was no greater saint of God. We will always remember his 'Children, put on your faith glasses!' when the impossible trials hit us! Wow! Know what? It works!" — Paul F. Crouch

Paul Crouch, Jim Bakker, and Rod Henke were the original hosts of TBN's Praise the Lord.

(714) 731-1000

PRAISE THE LORD
P.O. Box A
Santa Ana, CA 92711

The TBN family rejoices during early Praise-a-Thons.

God Moves a Mountain

T he station God provided to begin the miracle of TBN turned out to be a non-operational UHF station the FCC warned had to be back on the air by May 28, 1973. But as Paul and his team of engineers raced to meet the deadline they faced a major obstacle. Something was blocking TBN's studio signal from reaching its transmitter 50 miles away on Mt. Wilson. Sure enough, experts confirmed that there was no way for a signal to get through because a piece of the mountain stood in the way.

While all seemed lost, Paul soon found himself climbing the ladder to the roof of the studio where the transmitter dish was installed. With tears rolling down his face Paul stretched out his hand to touch the dish and pour out his heart to the Lord: "Father, You said if we had faith the size of a mustard seed, we could say to a mountain, 'Be removed and be cast into the sea,' and it would go." As Paul laid out TBN's desperate need, a sense of God's presence enveloped him,

"and I knew my heavenly Father had answered."

Paul hurried back down to the studio and asked the weary engineers to give it one more try the next day, a Sunday. And so at eight o'clock that Sabbath morning they gathered in the studio control room, but this time with expectancy in the air as the transformers warmed up and the chief engineer phoned his man stationed at TBN's antenna on Mt. Wilson. Suddenly there was a shout from over the phone as the engineer exclaimed with astonishment: "We've got the picture! And it's as clear as NBC!"

Everyone in the room knew they had seen a miracle. "We were all witnesses, including the engineers, who were by no means Christians," said Paul. "God had moved a mountain for us—and not just a figurative one, but one made out of dirt and rock. And ever since then, TBN's crystal-clear signal has continued to pass through the 'cleft in the rock' God provided for us."

Paul Crouch's 1973 executive planner opened to May 28 — TBN's miraculous launch! "It's a good thing my dad was a pack rat, because he pulled this planner out to show us all the intense planning — and prayer — that went in to getting and keeping TBN on the air."
— Matt Crouch

On May 28, 1973, TBN signed on the air with excitement and anticipation. "We were only broadcasting a few hours a day," recalled Paul, "but the calls we got from viewers made us feel like we were on top of the TV ratings."

Exuberant praise was a hallmark of TBN Praise-a-Thons.

"It was so exciting to watch as our precious partners called in to help us reach our goals." – Jan Crouch

TBN's first Praise-a-Thon, October 1973.

TBN's own Spirit Song joined Betty Jean Robinson, Walt Mills — and Jan on the vibraharp — during an early Praise-a-Thon. "Once we warmed up, it was hard to get us to stop. One man actually called in and made a large pledge — if we STOPPED playing!" – Jan Crouch

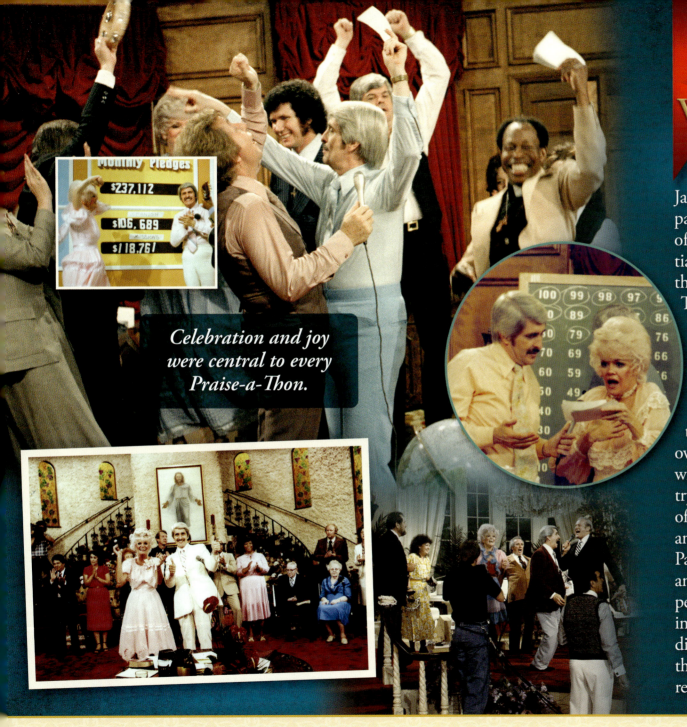

Celebration and joy were central to every Praise-a-Thon.

Trial by Fire

While Christians and many church leaders in the Los Angeles area enthusiastically supported TBN, Paul and Jan soon realized that some local pastors were antagonistic to the idea of a TV station devoted to Christian programming. "Looking back I think these men of God were afraid TBN would compete with their vision and drain finances away from their works," recalled Paul.

In addition, there were other church leaders who realized the potential of Christian television and tried to take control of TBN for their own benefit. One prominent pastor whose church had its own TV ministry was so insistent upon being a part of TBN that he maneuvered to take an active role in its direction, offering Paul the use of the church's cameras and equipment — which TBN desperately needed but couldn't afford — in return for a seat on TBN's board of directors. "Deep in our heart we knew the arrangement was not God's best," recalled Paul. "But we were at a cross-roads and this seemed like the only way to move ahead."

As Paul and Jan began looking to others rather than God for direction, His blessing began to lift. Three months after it had signed on with such promise, something happened that threatened to silence TBN. Paul had been negotiating with the owner to purchase the station, but as TBN struggled each month just to pay for air time, the owner lost hope that Paul would be able to come up with the down payment required for purchase, and began to look for another buyer.

"One day we learned that the owner had struck a deal with an area pastor to buy the station right out from under us," recalled Paul, "and within the next 30 days we would be off the air."

With hopes dashed and the end of his and Jan's dream apparently at hand, Paul walked out of his office that afternoon with tears flowing freely and his heart broken. "It looked like the end of TBN," he said.

But God had other plans!

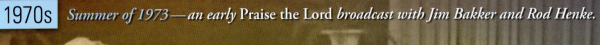

the tbn news

Vol. 1 - No. 1   Trinity Broadcasting Network   111 W. Dyer Rd., Santa Ana, California 92707   October, 1973

"and every eye shall see 'him'"

by Paul Crouch

One of the great secrets hidden in the Bible for centuries is the miracle of TV and radio.

The Psalmist David never dreamed in his wildest imagination that man would one day send his voice through thin air at the speed of light. Yet the Holy Spirit knew this as He inspired David to write: "There is no speech nor language where their voice is not heard.

is it possible ?

by Jim Bakker

How exciting it is to live daily in the midst of a miracle! Only God could build a television network in just a few short weeks.

As I write to you today, Trinity Broadcasting Network is just a little over four months old and has the potential of reaching nearly twenty million people.

TRINITY BROADCASTING SYSTEMS ANNOUNCES, SOUTHERN CALIFORNIA'S NEWEST CHRISTIAN TELEVISION STATION...

CHANNEL

46 KBSA-TV

ON THE AIR TO...

praise THE **lord**

"We were proud of our very first video recorder, a nearly out-of-date 'reel to reel' machine as big as a small car. By contrast today's digital recorders will fit in one hand." –Paul F. Crouch

TBN's first kids' show featured Jan (right) and Tammy Bakker.

the new **JIM** and **TAMMY** **SHOW**

A New Beginning

With no station and no prospects, Paul and Jan Crouch were driven to their knees over the future of TBN. It wasn't long before Paul heard the voice of the Lord say, "Call Angel Lerma." Angel was a local businessman who owned Channel 40 and had turned down previous inquiries. When Paul called he learned Angel had decided that day to sell the station—for $1 million. While that was an impossible amount for the Crouches, he offered to finance the sale with only $100,000 up front.

"I didn't even take a moment before agreeing," recalled Paul. "Miraculously, within two weeks we had made a successful switch to the new station, which had four times the power and double the population coverage."

Even as God blessed, however, the pastor who had maneuvered his way on to TBN's board mounted a last-ditch effort to gain control, and it was only through God's intervention that his efforts were blocked and he was removed from the board. With his departure, Paul and Jan were forced to turn to God as the deadline for the $100,000 down payment on TBN's new station loomed only days away.

But on the day of the deadline they were still $35,000 short and faced the loss of the station by 3 p.m. at the end of the business day. As the clock passed 2:30 that afternoon TBN's first couple cried out to God for another miracle.

That miracle arrived minutes before the deadline in the person of Scotty Scotvold, a strange little man who explained that he had been planning to buy a new yacht when God told him to sow the money into TBN instead. With that, Mr. Scotvold handed Paul a folded paper that turned out to be a check—for $35,000.

"My eyes filled with tears as I accepted the precious seed sown by this unusual man sent in the nick of time by God," recalled Paul. "And as I raced out the door and to the bank, making it just in time, my heart was filled with thanksgiving to God for His faithfulness in bringing us through another crisis."

> "God will often wait until the last moment to answer your prayer so there is no doubt who brought you through."
> – Paul F. Crouch

> "**S**cotty Scotvold. Dear, dear Scotty — how can we thank you, honor you, bless you for obeying our Lord that fateful day? Yes, Scotty Scotvold, my dear Lutheran brother, came 'in the fullness of time' (Galatians 4:4). One half hour before the bank closed, Scotty pressed a check into my hand. That $35,000 made the $100,000 down payment for station number one — Channel 40. Scotty remained my dear friend and TBN partner until his homegoing at age 92." — Paul F. Crouch

August 2nd is a historic date for TBN. On August 2, 1973, Trinity Broadcasting Network was formed as a corporation. Exactly one year later the FCC granted the license for KTBN-TV 40, TBN's first station.

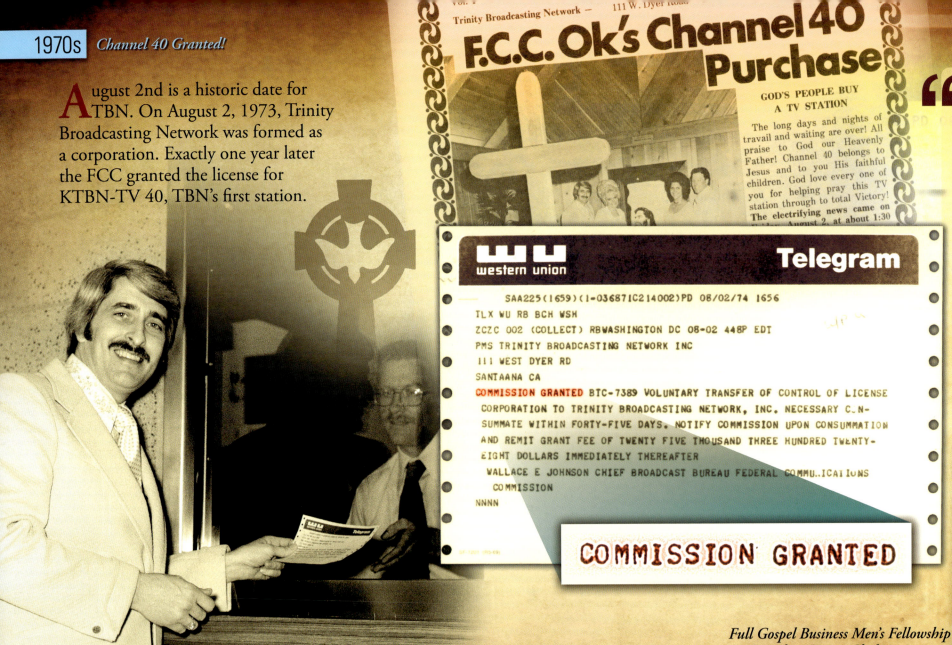

Trinity Broadcasting Network — 111 W. Dyer Road

F.C.C. Ok's Channel 40 Purchase

GOD'S PEOPLE BUY A TV STATION

The long days and nights of travail and waiting are over! All praise to God our Heavenly Father! Channel 40 belongs to Jesus and to you His faithful children. God love every one of you for helping pray this TV station through to total Victory! The electrifying news came on ... August 2, at about 1:30

Telegram

western union

SAA225(1659)(1-036871C214002)PD 08/02/74 1656
TLX WU RB BCH WSH
ZCZC 002 (COLLECT) RBWASHINGTON DC 08-02 448P EDT
PMS TRINITY BROADCASTING NETWORK INC
111 WEST DYER RD
SANTAANA CA
COMMISSION GRANTED BTC-7389 VOLUNTARY TRANSFER OF CONTROL OF LICENSE
CORPORATION TO TRINITY BROADCASTING NETWORK, INC. NECESSARY CON-
SUMMATE WITHIN FORTY-FIVE DAYS. NOTIFY COMMISSION UPON CONSUMMATION
AND REMIT GRANT FEE OF TWENTY FIVE THOUSAND THREE HUNDRED TWENTY-
EIGHT DOLLARS IMMEDIATELY THEREAFTER
WALLACE E JOHNSON CHIEF BROADCAST BUREAU FEDERAL COMMU..ICATIONS
COMMISSION
NNNN

COMMISSION GRANTED

GOD BLESS WESTERN UNION!

> "Oh, what a day! August 2, 1974. We had cried, fasted, and prayed. We pled with our TV partners to help with the $100,000 down payment. Finally, the FCC telegram came! I raced to the Western Union office to personally pick up the most beautiful piece of paper that confirmed KTBN-TV Channel 40 was ours in Jesus' name! That night, the *Praise the Lord* program was truly 'joy unspeakable and full of glory!' Wow — walk on water!" — Paul F. Crouch

Full Gospel Business Men's Fellowship President Demos Shakarian was a frequent guest on Praise the Lord.

CHANNEL 40 BELONGS TO GOD'S PEOPLE

Marv Martin, Chico Holiday, Walt Mills, and Roger McDuff in 1978.

Ministry partner Jack Hayford.

Paul and Jenny Billheimer were among TBN's early programmers and led the way on teaching about the power of prayer.

The miracle of satellite has transitioned to global broadcast coverage through the Internet — what in essence is a worldwide cable system. Paul Crouch would be thrilled to see TBN programming available on billions of computers, smart phones, televisions — literally every electronic device across the earth!

Prophecy expert Dr. Charles Taylor.

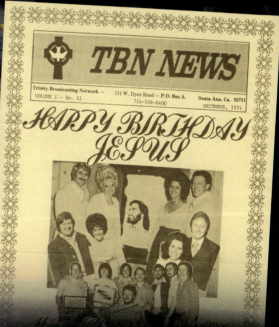

TBN NEWS

Trinity Broadcasting Network —   111 W. Dyer Road — P.O. Box A.   Santa Ana, Ca. 92711
VOLUME 1 — No. 11   714-556-8400
                                                                    DECEMBER, 1974

HAPPY BIRTHDAY JESUS

Anointing the "Big Dish" with Holy Land oil as TBN launches its first satellite TV station.

One of TBN's first production trucks for broadcasting live programming from remote locations.

Paul Crouch demonstrating to viewers how TBN's satellite earth station communicates with the terrestrial satellite.

> "I've never grown tired of talking about the miracle of satellite technology and how it has enabled us to send the gospel to literally every corner of the earth."
> — Paul F. Crouch

Paul Billheimer, one of TBN's earliest teachers and faithful ministry partners, offers a blessing during TBN's satellite dedication.

The Vision of Satellite TV

Through the miracle of satellite technology, TBN has been able to reach the nation—and the world—with life-changing Christian TV.

God called the Crouches to help take Christian TV to the nation and world, and in October 1975 He gave Paul a vision of how it would happen. As Paul waited on the Lord in prayer one afternoon, he suddenly saw a giant map of the U.S. stretch across the ceiling, and high above was an intensely bright glow from which issued forth fine streams of light, traveling down to outline the exterior of the map. "These streams of light targeted major coastal population centers," said Paul—"Los Angeles, Miami, New York, Seattle, and on and on—until the entire nation was outlined."

As these beams of light struck, smaller threads of light spread across the map, and soon Paul was conscious of little dots of intense light beginning to glow, until the whole map across the ceiling was bathed in an intricate network of beautiful lights. "I sat there before this magnificent vision from the Lord, utterly transfixed by what I was seeing," Paul recalled. "What did

> "In order to prepare you for your Promised Land, God must first move you out of your comfort zone."
> – Paul F. Crouch

it all mean? As I pondered and asked God about it, He responded with one resounding word spoken into my spirit: 'SATELLITE!'"

"But how, Lord, and when?" Paul asked, weeping. *"Soon,"* the Lord replied. *"Very soon."*

Paul soon got a call from an electronics giant that was preparing to launch one of the first TV satellites, and before long TBN had a contract and equipment for 24-hour satellite feed. But it would take months of agonizing delays and much concerted prayer before the FCC approved TBN for its first satellite station.

Finally, on April 10, 1978, Paul's vision came to fruition as TBN broadcast its first satellite transmission, beaming its *Praise the Lord* program to a convention in Las Vegas. Satellite quickly became a crucial part of TBN's broadcast distribution and eventually nearly 100 satellites fed the gospel around the world. Paul never forgot this amazing chain of events, stating, "I still consider this small beginning a mighty miracle."

From stations across America to networks all over the world, the miracle of satellite technology empowered TBN to send television programming just about everywhere. Recalled Paul: "Our dear partners were quick to see the benefit of this new tool, and they were on board immediately."

Sharing the vision of satellite broadcast during a Praise-a-Thon.

We were excited to share with partners about how satellite technology would enable TBN to send life-changing Christian television to people everywhere!

SATCOM III

RCA

Admit One
RCA American Communications
Blast Off Buffet

Arthur Blessitt with a model of "Angel II," the second satellite TBN accessed, linking all its stations together as a network.

Paul explains the miracle of satellite TV to viewers.

Satellite has given TBN a global impact.

Satellite channels feed TBN's networks to thousands of television stations, cable providers, and countless home satellite dishes worldwide, reaching a potential viewing audience of over one billion viewers. Today that miraculous technology has been joined by online apps and social media platforms to take TBN programming to the billions on earth with smart phones and electronic devices. Paul Crouch would be thrilled!

Big dish in South Africa, where TBN launched some of its first foreign stations.

TBN satellite feeds, like this giant dish in the Philippines, keep TBN programming on the air around the world.

In 1980, presenting Prime Minister Menachem Begin with a petition signed by hundreds of thousands of TBN friends and partners pledging their support for making Jerusalem the eternal capital of Israel.

O ver the span of 40 years, Paul and Jan met with nearly every Israeli prime minister, emphasizing to each the great love the church in America has for the land of God's people. Without exception, each Israeli leader expressed appreciation for the prayers and support believers—especially TBN's friends and partners—offered on behalf of their nation.

Meeting Prime Minister Benjamin Netanyahu in 2011.

With Prime Minister Benjamin Netanyahu.

January 2020, an exclusive TBN interview with Prime Minister Netanyahu.

With Prime Minister Shimon Peres.

Prime Minister Ariel Sharon.

A cordial meeting with Prime Minister Yitzhak Shamir.

COLOUR T.V.

3 I.TV
אולפני הרצליה
HERZLIYA STUDIOS

RCA

"The very first LIVE *Praise the Lord* from Israel! About 300 TBN partners helped to sing and shout God's glory, standing on the Mount of Olives. We did these historic programs three years in a row."

Over the years TBN has hosted and broadcast scores of special gatherings, concerts, rallies, and other events across the nation and around the world. And God has always been faithful to move as only He can, touching people with His love, hope, and grace.

Longtime ministry partner Jerry Barnard at one of TBN's revival meetings.

Howard and Vestal Goodman bring their Southern Gospel enthusiasm to a TBN rally.

James Robison offers a message of salvation.

Andraé Crouch sings one of his 1970s gospel favorites.

Jerry Barnard preaches an old-time Pentecostal message.

When TBN visited other cities for a rally, the day wasn't complete without a "March for Jesus" led by Arthur Blessitt.

"There has been no greater joy for us over the past forty years than the countless opportunities we have had to meet, pray, and fellowship with our many partners, friends, and fellow Christians. The early TBN rallies and gatherings were a vital part of what kept us pressing ahead when trials and obstacles threatened the vision God gave us. We'll never forget the many thousands of individuals and families who stood with us, held us up in prayer when we were weary, and believed with us for a kingdom harvest through Christian television."

— Paul and Jan Crouch

The "Holy Beamer" at one of its first remote broadcasts.

Jan Crouch prays through the inside of the "Holy Beamer" during its dedication.

Dedicating the "Holy Beamer on the 18-Wheeler": TBN ministry partner Oral Roberts (second from right) leads in prayer as the "Beamer" prepares for its first remote broadcast.

Ministry guests join Paul and Jan to pray over a model of the "Holy Beamer" during Praise the Lord.

An artist's rendering of the "Holy Beamer" at the 1984 Olympics.

> **"The engineers said it could not be done. But with God it not only WAS DONE, but our old-time partners saw the Holy Beamer as it rolled through most of these forty glorious years to virtually every corner of the USA! And guess what? We're still rolling — until !?!?"**
> — Paul F. Crouch

The "Holy Beamer"

With stations in Los Angeles and Phoenix and a satellite station poised to beam Christian TV coast-to-coast, Paul Crouch and the TBN team pursued every means that would aid them in TBN's broadcast mission. One of the most innovative tools was a mobile studio nicknamed the "Holy Beamer." Fully equipped with broadcast equipment, satellite dish, and uplink transmitter, the Holy Beamer was really a TV station on a tractor-trailer, enabling TBN to travel across America, bringing crusades, concerts, conventions, and other events right to TBN viewers.

> "God gives to those who ask, and the more we ask, in faith believing, the more He will pour into our lives."
> – Paul F. Crouch

The Holy Beamer arrived just in time for TBN to cover the 1980 Washington for Jesus rally, which brought nearly one million Americans together at the nation's Capital to pray for America's future. Later that year it rolled into Reno, Nevada for Billy Graham's historic four-night crusade, providing satellite feed to TBN's stations and other networks around the nation. "The idea of a mobile studio broadcasting live events was revolutionary for Christian media," recalled Paul. "But God gave us the vision to understand that advances in technology were open doors for the extension of His kingdom."

In the next few years TBN added additional mobile trucks, giving us the capability to be on the road almost constantly, covering Christian events, producing special broadcasts, and giving TBN's growing audience an exclusive connection to what was happening in the body of Christ.

As a young man helping his parents in the growing Christian network, Matt Crouch got plenty of hands-on experience with the emerging technology that was giving TBN a broadcast edge. "The Holy Beamer rigs enabled TBN to produce a greater variety of programs," recalled Matt. "From on-site *Praise the Lord* segments, to whole programs shot remotely across America, these mobile units revolutionized what we were able to bring to Christian television."

"No one could do it better than R. W. Schambach! 'Don't touch that dial until you hear my testimony!' he'd shout as he pointed into the camera. 'I was running home as I passed an old street preacher. I heard him cry, 'Hey Sinner!' I stopped to wonder, 'How does he know me?' So I listened long enough until I found my knees on hard concrete accepting Jesus as my Savior and Lord! Now I cry, 'Hey Sinner!' — Paul F. Crouch"

Kenneth Hagin and Oral Roberts, two twentieth-century giants of the faith, were TBN viewer favorites.

"Don't touch that dial, sinner!"
– R. W. Schambach

Kenneth Copeland's message of faith blessed viewers for many years.

Evangelist T. L. Osborn always brought a word of hope and encouragement to TBN viewers.

James Robison challenges viewers to step into all that Christ has provided.

Dwight Thompson's bold message of salvation and deliverance touched the lives of millions.

> "God has done all He will ever do about the devil! Now it is up to us to ENFORCE HIS VICTORY over that evil one! Has he stolen from you? I'm sure he has! Take it back in Jesus' name! A million of you said, 'Amen!' as we rejoiced and rallied at 'Washington for Jesus' in 1980. Yes, we've taken some back, but there's lots more to do. So, Go! Go! Go!"
>
> — Paul F. Crouch

Washington for JESUS

Paul Crouch
Trinity Broadcasting

GUEST

Gathered for prayer before the rally were Pastor Adrian Rogers, Paul, Bill Bright, Pastor E.V. Hill, Pastor D. James Kennedy, Jan.

TBN broadcast the "Washington for Jesus" rally live from the nation's Capital.

Paul addresses the over one million Americans gathered at the Capitol Mall for "Washington for Jesus."

Trinity Broadcasting Network

Washington For Jesus | April 29, 1980

"**O**ver one million of us met on the National Mall in Washington, D.C. We prayed that God would bless America and send an earth-shattering revival. My word was simply, 'God has done all He is going to do about the devil. Now it is up to us to enforce His victory. Yes, now it is up to us to take back all that the enemy has stolen from us in Jesus' name!'"
— Paul F. Crouch

Interviewing First Lady Rosalynn Carter at the White House.

> "**D**uring one of our 1980s Praise-a-Thons we displayed a big U.S. map with signs representing all of TBN's full-power stations. If we had a map today representing every place on earth where we have a station, we'd need a map the size of Texas!"
>
> — Paul F. Crouch

ON TO INDIANA, OHIO, KENTUCKY!

WTBY CHANNEL 54 NEW YORK

Rejoicing over another milestone as we symbolically "flip the switch" on a new station.

Through Dr. Lester Sumrall's generosity TBN was able to purchase his Miami station, which became TBN's third full-power station.

Power Surge for the Gospel

With Channel 40 in Los Angeles, the launch of Channel 21 in Phoenix, and hundreds of new cable stations, thanks to emerging satellite technology, TBN surged forward dramatically, logging over 250,000 decisions for Christ by the end of 1979. The next year a third station came aboard with the purchase of WHFT, Channel 45, in Miami, Florida. "The addition of Channel 45 meant that TBN now had a powerful presence for Christian television on both coasts," explained Paul. "What a night it was in July of 1980, when we threw the first coast-to-coast switch and linked East and West together — live — for the first time in the history of Christian TV."

The year 1980 also saw TBN's salvation tally rise to 700,000, and to the miraculous one million mark by the end of 1981. Over the next three years God blessed us with four additional full-power TBN stations broadcasting to over 20 million potential viewers.

The first was KTBO, Channel 14, in Oklahoma City, which signed on the air in March 1981. That was followed in July 1982 by WTBY, Channel 54, in Poughkeepsie, New York. Less than a month after the launch of the New York channel, Paul and Jan were in Richmond, Indiana for the launch in August of WKOI, Channel 43, which covered Cincinnati and the surrounding suburbs, as well as parts of Indiana and Kentucky.

In March 1984 TBN added its seventh station as KTBW, Channel 20, began broadcasting to the greater Seattle and Tacoma areas, reaching a potential of over three million viewers.

Paul recalled: "In a little over ten years, God had taken TBN from one small station on the air a couple of hours each night, to seven stations coast-to-coast broadcasting round-the-clock Christian programming that was changing lives. We would be the first to testify that this expansion had little to do with us. It was all God working through our weakness to make His glory known."

> "... this expansion had little to do with us. It was all God working through our weakness to make His glory known."
> – Paul F. Crouch

Sharing a special moment during one of the large Christian events TBN covered during the early years.

Studying the Word was always an important part of Praise the Lord.

Paul and Jan at TBN's Oklahoma City TV tower in 1981.

Praise The Lord
JUNE 1980
MIAMI-GRANTED
Beloved TBN Family:

Praise THE LORD
24 Hour Christian Television
VOLUME IX NO.III — MARCH 1980
OKLAHOMA "ON THE AIR" CHANNEL 14
Beloved T.V. Partner:

Praise The Lord
VOL. X NO. V — JUNE 1982
CINCINNATI-RICHMOND-DAYTON ON THE AIR!!

Praise The Lord
AUGUST 1982
NEW LIGHT IN NEW YORK

Praise The Lord
VOL. XI NO. 2 — JANUARY 1983
SEATTLE/TACOMA — STATION NUMBER SEVEN!!!

One of Jan's favorite TBN duties was to count and pray over the daily salvation reports received from the prayer partners.

On July 29, 1977, TBN was with evangelist Arthur Blessitt on famed Sunset Boulevard for a spontaneous event that came to be known as Hallelujah Hollywood.

"It's no stretch to say that for many years on any day of the week, somewhere in the world there was at least one TBN tower or station being constructed." –Paul F. Crouch

Sharing excitement with viewers over reaching another miraculous goal.

Multiple Grammy Award winning gospel singer and songwriter Andraé Crouch.

On hand for a Full Gospel Business Men's Fellowship event.

Speaking with friends and partners at one of the many Los Angeles-area TBN gatherings.

Gene Neill shared how he went from being a high-powered Florida attorney to an inmate in federal prison — and how Jesus changed everything.

Paul and Jan begin a Praise the Lord *program with an enthusiastic audience.*

100 STATIONS ON THE WAY!

One of TBN's popular early
ministry partners, Dr. E.V. Hill,
joined Paul and Jan in prayer
over a new full-power station.

*In 1984, during a
Praise the Lord broadcast,
Oral Roberts prayed over Jan
as she was preparing to
join the board of regents at
Oral Roberts University.*

TBN's miracle antenna and tower in Miami, Florida. Recalled Paul: "As the forty-foot-long, three-ton antenna was being put into place by helicopter, the cable released too soon. But God held it steady in a heavy wind until the engineers could bolt it down properly. And, for nearly 40 years that antenna has been beaming the gospel up and down the Gold Coast of Florida!"

Jan discusses her Smile of a Child Christmas toy drive on a Praise the Lord *broadcast.*

Pat Boone was a frequent Praise the Lord *guest.*

Dale Evans, a TBN viewer favorite, on a Praise the Lord *program in the 1980s.*

Camera crane operator Randy Layson looks down on Studio C.

Staff at WHFT, TBN's Miami, Florida station.

Beloved pastors and evangelists Paul and Jenny Billheimer (center) spent their final years at TBN. Said Paul: "Mom and Dad Billheimer, as we called them, taught us more about prayer than anyone in the world."

Interviewing Nora Lam, whose dramatic story of imprisonment in China and her escape to the West is the subject of the award-winning TBN movie China Cry.

Los Angeles Mayor Tom Bradley was an extra special guest on Praise the Lord.

Arthur Blessitt, Billy Graham, Jan and Paul, and Ruth Graham at Billy's 1980 Reno, Nevada crusade.

Enjoying a moment at Billy Graham's Reno, Nevada crusade.

" **E**arly *Praise the Lord* programs brought thousands of souls into the Kingdom. Hal Lindsey (right) surely taught us Bible prophecy and the nearness of the coming of the Lord! Each white slip of paper represented a soul coming to faith in Jesus. This was our TV altar call. "

— Paul F. Crouch

TO THE ISLANDS OF THE SEA

Dedication of TBN's first international station in the Caribbean island nation of Nevis-St. Kitts.

EUROPE! HERE WE COME!

"**H**ELLO WORLD INDEED! I have often said that I feel like the general who got on his horse and rode off in all directions at once! This early shot from somewhere near the North Pole graphically expresses the TBN vision to reach the whole wide world! By the way, it was 60 degrees below zero when this picture was taken! — Paul F. Crouch"

Rejoicing over another international TV station!

Paul and Matt in 1982 on an Israel-sponsored tour of Beirut, Lebanon.

Signpost directions:
- North Pole 3 hrs. 15 min.
- Copenhagen 4 hrs. 15 min.
- Los Angeles 6 hrs. 45 min.
- New York 4 hrs.
- Moscow 5 hrs. 20 min.
- Tokyo 10 hrs. 05 min.
- Frankfurt 4 hrs. 40 min.
- London 3 hrs. 35 min.

To the World!

From the beginning Paul and Jan's dream was to use television to reach the world for Christ. In the late 1970s TBN began sending programming to Central America and as far away as Indonesia, but their prayer was to establish brick-and-mortar stations on foreign soil.

God began answering that prayer in 1984 when TBN launched its first foreign station in the tiny Caribbean nation of Nevis-St. Kitts. "Some laughed at this small start," recalled Paul, "but we saw it as a down payment on God's promise to use TV in a global harvest."

Major doors opened later that year when TBN began beaming programming via satellite throughout Europe and North Africa, followed by the launch of its first European station in Italy. By 1985 TBN had three Italian stations broadcasting to over seven million.

In 1987 Africa became the focus when Ciskei opened its doors to the first African station. "Where missionaries once traveled weeks to preach to a few small villages," said Paul, "today several TBN networks broadcast the gospel throughout this once 'dark continent.'"

Latin America was also a priority, and Paul redoubled his efforts after seeing the desperate situation in war-torn El Salvador. Following several years of prayer and labor, a light burst through the darkness as TBN launched its first station in that country in the early 1990s, as well as in Belize and Costa Rica.

In August 1992, TBN added a station in war-tattered Nicaragua, giving the kingdom of God another victory over the powers of darkness. "The apostle Paul tells us that as we take territory for God's kingdom, we are not wrestling against flesh and blood, but against 'spiritual hosts of wickedness,'" said Paul. "We were able to attest to the truth of that scripture as we added these gospel lights in Central America. We were driven to our knees often as station after station came on the air."

> "Jesus calls each of us as believers to take His passion and love for the world as our own."
> – Paul F. Crouch

Paul, Jan, and Laurie meet Queen Elizabeth II.

Central America was the focus of one of TBN's first expansions outside the U.S. Paul and Jan found the people in each of the countries hungry for the gospel and more of God. "It was prime territory for Christian television," said Paul.

HONDURAS GRANTED

Setting up an antenna for TBN's Costa Rica station.

Paul visited El Salvador to help launch a new TBN station there.

Rejoicing over TBN's launch in Costa Rica.

Italy, We've Got You Covered!

Greeting TBN viewers in Italy.

Hal Lindsey, Paul Crouch, Chuck Hall, and Norm Juggert at the Milan, Italy station.

An in-studio translator provides Italian voice-over for one of the ministry programs TBN provides to TCI.

Another meeting to promote Christian television in Italy.

Under TBN's broadcast tower in Rome.

T BN's Italian network, Televisione Cristiana in Italia (TCI), has been on the air since 1985, when Paul purchased a station in Campione d'Italia, a small piece of Italian land surrounded by Switzerland. That channel began to broadcast life-changing Christian programing throughout northern Italy. The addition of two more stations soon after meant that seven million Italian-speaking viewers could receive the good news of Jesus through television.

Fast forward nearly forty years and today, through a national Italian broadcast license and carrier arrangement acquired by TBN, TCI's reach has expanded dramatically to give 96 percent of Italy's more than 60 million residents round-the-clock access to culturally relevant, life-changing Christian programming.

"In this land that represented the epicenter of the early Christian faith, the message of hope and grace through Jesus is now available to literally every Italian home and heart through TBN," said Matt Crouch. "We're believing for a massive harvest of souls for Italy and beyond."

From actors and singers to businessmen, politicians, and ministry leaders, everyone enjoyed being a guest on *Praise the Lord*. The warm welcome, laid-back atmosphere, and friendly fellowship was a joy to guests and viewers alike.

Praise the Lord host James Robison welcomed guest Charles Stanley.

Pat Boone hosted many Praise the Lord *programs over the years.*

(From top left) Smokey Robinson, Andraé Crouch, John Wimber, C.M. Ward, and Rex Humbard all stopped by to praise the Lord.

Pat Robertson and Oral Roberts on a Praise the Lord *broadcast from ORU.*

Former Miss America Cheryl Prewitt-Salem.

Oral Roberts brings an encouraging word to the Praise the Lord *audience.*

Ricky Skaggs brought his down-home country charm.

Actor Gavin MacLeod and his wife Patti on Praise the Lord.

Beloved actor Dean Jones and his lovely wife Lory were frequent guests and part of the TBN family for years.

Dale Evans and Roy Rogers gave TBN autographed momentos from their movie days.

Debbie Boone lights up the Praise the Lord set with her anointed singing.

Evangelist Reinhard Bonnke passionately declaring "Africa shall be saved!"

Rex Humbard was a regular guest and a friend of TBN for many years.

John Wimber on Praise the Lord.

Enjoying a moment with Mr. T and Rosey Grier.

"Something good is going to happen to you"—Oral Roberts and his lovely wife Evelyn encourage viewers.

Betty Jean Robinson was a longtime viewer favorite.

Dale and Roy brought back memories with their signature song, "Happy Trails to You."

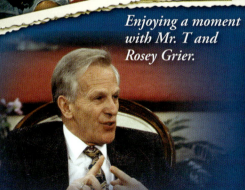

Brother Andrew, "God's Smuggler," took thousands of Bibles to believers in communist countries and other oppressed areas.

R. W. Schambach never failed to light up the prayer lines with people needing salvation.

For years, actor Efrem Zimbalist, Jr. was the "golden voice" of TBN's station breaks.

Dr. David Yonggi Cho, Korean pastor of the largest church in the world, with a membership of over one million.

Dean and Mary Brown were longtime Praise the Lord *hosts.*

Popular Christian singer Karen Wheaton.

With singer Candi Staton.

Basketball great Meadowlark Lemon was a TBN friend for many years.

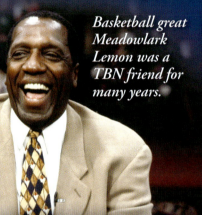

David du Plessis, "Mr. Pentecost," ministered powerfully on the Holy Spirit.

Rosey Grier, legendary member of the LA Rams' "Fearsome Foursome" as well as an impacting minister and TBN partner.

Dr. Lloyd John Ogilvie shared about a move of God in his church, Hollywood Presbyterian.

Steve Brock, Roger McDuff, and Ben Kinchlow, three TBN regulars.

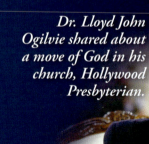

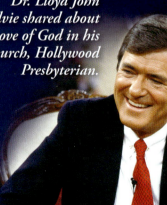

Casey Treat, a popular TBN ministry partner.

Rich and Robyn Wilkerson

E.V. Hill ministered powerfully on many Praise the Lord *programs.*

*Mario Murillo has preached the gospel
all over the world.*

*Evangelist Nicky Cruz and gospel singer-song-
writer Andraé Crouch share their love for Jesus.*

*Oral Roberts and Jack Hayford, two elder
statesmen of Pentecost.*

*Nora Lam's life was the
subject of the TBN movie*
China Cry. *Nora was
a frequent guest on TBN.*

*Kenneth Hagin always
had an anointed word of
faith for TBN viewers.*

*Vonette and Bill
Bright, founders of
Campus Crusade
for Christ.*

*Actress Debra Paget, star of the Hollywood big-screen
epic* The Ten Commandments.

HITHERTO HAVE YE ASKED NOTHING...ASK!

...he seventy returned with joy, saying, "Lord, even the demons are subject to us in your **NAME**!

Matt Crouch proposed to Laurie Orndorff on the air (she said yes).

Matt and Laurie chose the famed Crystal Cathedral for their August 25, 1985, wedding.

Paul and Jan Crouch tied the knot August 25, 1957, in Columbus, Georgia.

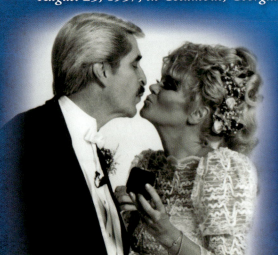

Mark and Diane Yasuhara, The Hawaiians, were frequent musical guests.

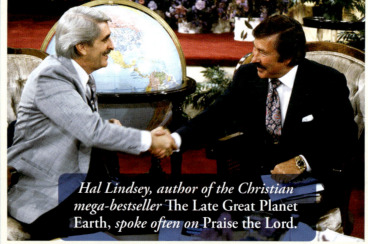

Hal Lindsey, author of the Christian mega-bestseller The Late Great Planet Earth, *spoke often on* Praise the Lord.

Praise The Lord

VOL. XIII NO. VIII — TRINITY BROADCASTING NETWORK — AUGUST 19..

THE GOOD NEWS JUST WON'T QUIT!!

Paul spoke at the Billy Graham Crusade in Anaheim, California.

Dr. Billy Graham, a longtime friend of the Crouches and TBN.

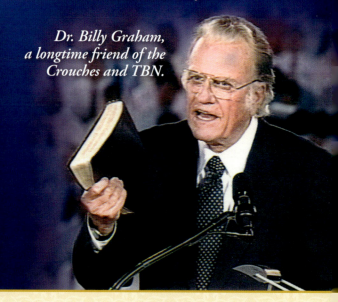

In prayer over viewer needs.

The Lord

TRINITY BROADCASTING NETWORK   VOL. XIII NO. XII DECEMBER 1988

"THANKS BE UNTO GOD...

FOR HIS UNSPEAKABLE GIFT." II Cor. 9:15

POSSESSING THE KINGDOM!

LET MY PEOPLE GO!

Ray Charles sings *"Little Drummer Boy"* on the 1986 Worldwide Christmas Special.

GADSDEN—BIRMINGHAM—ON THE AIR!

Enjoying a light moment during a Praise the Lord *broadcast.*

Sharing a verse to encourage TBN viewers.

As TBN expanded its satellite reach, one unique love gift reminded partners to pray for God's blessing over this "miracle" technology.

As TBN spread across the country it was important to visit supporters in new areas. So the *Praise the Lord* program often went on the road to churches and auditoriums. The Lord moved and many classic moments happened as the TBN family got together.

A few of the special moments on the road with TBN: Paul and Jan encourage an audience (left) and minister with TBN partners like R.W. Schambach (below).

Dean and Mary Brown

Meadowlark Lemon always brought down the house with his basketball tricks.

Paul and Jan join Arthur Blessitt at Gazzarri's night club on Sunset Boulevard in Hollywood.

There were great times of refreshing, with anointed music and preaching.

In prayer at a TBN rally.

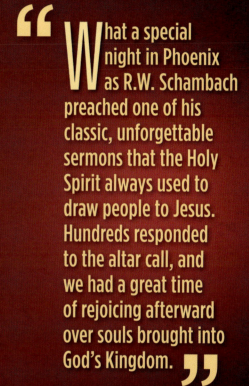

"What a special night in Phoenix was R.W. Schambach preached one of his classic, unforgettable sermons that the Holy Spirit always used to draw people to Jesus. Hundreds responded to the altar call, and we had a great time of rejoicing afterward over souls brought into God's Kingdom. "

— Paul F. Crouch

"To demonstrate the power of satellite technology, on Easter Day in 1992 TBN televised four sunrise services in four separate locations. Here Jan and I are leading one of those services, at the Hollywood Bowl in Hollywood, California. Only eternity will reveal the vast numbers of individuals from all across the earth whose lives were transformed because they were able to turn on a television set and hear the glorious message of the resurrected King of kings."

— Paul F. Crouch

HOLLYWOOD BOWL

TBN Easter sunrise service at the Hollywood Bowl.

Praise The Lord

TRINITY BROADCASTING NETWORK VOL. XIX, NO. III MARCH 1992

A NEW DOCTRINE!

...HATE this one, but WE ARE GOING TO LOVE IT! Our NEW DOCTRINE has ...theological doctrine or denomination! Besides, the...

Praise the Lord

NOVEMBER 1992
VOLUME XIX · NUMBER XI

Paul, Jan and Nicaraguan President Violeta

NICARAGUA ON THE AIR

"LISTEN! YOUR WATCHMEN LIFT UP THEIR VOICES, THEY SHO...
JOYFULLY TOGETHER; *FOR THEY WILL SEE WITH THEIR OWN E...
SALVATION OF OUR GOD...*
GLORIOUS GOOD N...

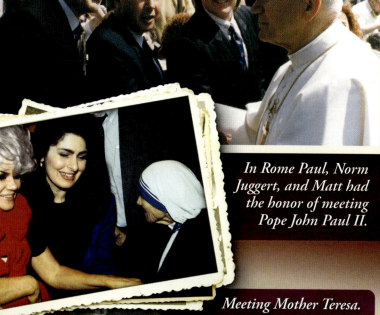

In Rome Paul, Norm Juggert, and Matt had the honor of meeting Pope John Paul II.

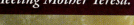

Meeting Mother Teresa.

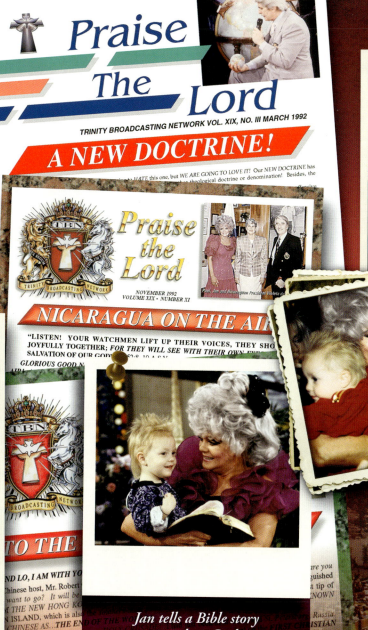

Jan tells a Bible story to grandson Caylan.

Paul and Jan look out across the audience of worshippers during TBN's Easter sunrise service at the Hollywood Bowl.

...ND LO, I AM WITH YO...
...Chinese host, Mr. Robert...
...want to go? It will be...
...THE NEW HONG KO...
...ISLAND, which is also...
...CHINESE AS...THE EN...
By now this journey had become...
Instead of heading back home, it...
TV STATION for the People's R...
little aircraft – EAGLE I – was forbidden to fly over China and...
dropped off in Helsinki, Finland and caught a flight to Tokyo, *then* on to Hong Kong, the final jumping off place...
for Hainan Island. But in Hong Kong we found that only two little commuter airlines flew to Haikou City, the...
Capitol of the southern-most province of Mainland China. DRAGON-AIR...

Paul and Oral Roberts pray over needs.

Andraé Crouch leads in worship.

Paul, Jan, and friends join legendary songwriter Dottie Rambo on one of her many gospel classics.

Husband-and-wife pop stars of the 1970s, Marilyn McCoo and Billy Davis Jr.

Father and son pastors, Matthew and Tommy Barnett.

Oral Roberts ministered life to viewers.

Glen Campbell shares a song.

Author and Christian apologist Josh McDowell.

With renowned Ten Commandments actor Charlton Heston.

Charles Blake, Presiding Bishop of the Church of God in Christ.

The legendary Dino accompanies Gary McSpadden, Cheryl Kartsonakis, Sandi Patty, and Larnelle Harris.

Pastor Ed Smith, a part of the
TBN family since 1973.

Paul Crouch leads a victory shout
on Praise the Lord.

Caylan and Cody with
eight-time Mr. Olympia,
Lee Haney.

Former Miss America, Cheryl Prewitt Salem.

Dr. Reginald Cherry brought fresh
perspectives on health.

TBN ministry partner Walt Mills
(center) leads in prayer.

Actresses Tia and Tamera Mowry, stars of
the hit show Sister, Sister.

Former NFL star Mike Barber.

Jerry Barnard, Dwight Thompson, and Paul.

TBN attorney and board member Colby May.

Bill Bright, founder of Campus
Crusade for Christ, with wife Vonette.

The wife of Hollywood icon Cary Grant and a talented actress in her own right, Dyan Cannon has also been outspoken about her love for the Lord.

"She finally got him! Yes, sweet Dale Evans coaxed Roy Rogers to come and give his testimony on *Praise the Lord*. We even got them to sing 'Happy Trails'! Wow — I even got to try on his famous cowboy hat! What a night! Sweet, sweet memories."
— Paul F. Crouch

Paul with good friend and TBN ministry partner Dr. Robert Schuller.

"The Bible says that 'Righteousness exalts a nation, but sin is a reproach to any people' (Proverbs 14:34). The heart of a national leader often reflects the spiritual condition of a country. That is why we must lift up our leaders in prayer. Many times we've seen hearts soften and doors open to the gospel and to TBN's influence in a country when we've prayed for that country's leaders. — Paul F. Crouch "

Dr. Crouch had the opportunity to interview South African President Nelson Mandela. "He was gracious and thankful for the gift of Christian television to the people of South Africa," recalled Paul.

DISHES, DISHES, DISHES!

Looking across the rooftops of Portugal over a sea of satellite dishes, Paul Crouch Sr. exclaimed, "Satellites, satellites, satellites!" He was right then and the same holds true today. Direct-to-Home satellite is still how hundreds of millions of viewers across the earth receive their television signals—including life-changing TBN programming. The rooftops of homes and apartment complexes in the Middle East, Latin America, and the Far East don't look appreciably different today than they did when Dr. Crouch was regularly traveling to those areas in his day. Satellite dishes are still a common sight. That's why TBN continues to strategically distribute Christian networks in 17 languages via satellite, over-the-air broadcast, cable, and digital platforms.

AUGUST 1993
VOLUME XX NUMBER VIII

AVAILABLE NOW
ON ALL DEVICES

android

tv

firetv

TBN

ALL THE FAITH-FILLED
CONTENT YOU LOVE

androidtv

Roku

*Millions view TBN's life-changing
content via online apps and platforms.*

*Rex Humbard leads a prayer
for the nations.*

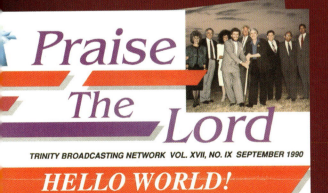

Praise
The
Lord

TRINITY BROADCASTING NETWORK   VOL. XVII, NO. IX   SEPTEMBER 1990

HELLO WORLD!

SING UNTO THE LORD, ALL THE EARTH; SHOW FORTH FROM DAY TO
DAY HIS SALVATION. DECLARE HIS GLORY AMONG THE HEATHEN: HIS
MARVELOUS WORKS AMONG ALL NATIONS." 1 Chronicles 16:23, 24

Miracles Across the Earth

L ooking back on the decade of the 1990s, it's clear to see those were the initial years of exponential, global expansion for TBN, as God rapidly opened doors in Latin America, Europe, and Africa. That's about the time the government of South Africa approved an entire TBN affiliate network to cover the nation with Christian programming. By the early 1990s TBN was on the air throughout Central and South America. In December 1996 Enlace, TBN's Spanish-language affiliate network, came to life, giving tens of millions of viewers in over 30 Spanish-speaking countries throughout Latin America instant access to Christian programming for the whole family. Six years later Enlace expanded into the U.S. to the approximately 62 million Hispanics (19% of the U.S. population) living in America.

But that was only the beginning. "God commands us to ask for the nations," said the late Paul Crouch. "We have taken Him at His Word,

> "God has faithfully answered our prayer to 'ask for the nations....'"
> – Matt Crouch

and He has honored our request many times over the past 40 years."

In the decades since the '90s, TBN's international reach has literally exploded, as we've added channels and networks like TBN UK, TBN Africa, TBN Asia, TBN Nordic, TBN Polska, five Middle Eastern networks, TBN España, Bibel TV in Germany, two powerful networks in Brazil, Life TV Estonia reaching much of Russia and Eastern Europe, digital networks for Ukraine and France, and many more coming online and on the air every year.

Most of TBN's domestic and international networks are available live over what has become the largest digital broadcast system in the world — the Internet. Through digital apps like Pluto, Freevee, Roku, Apple TV, YouTube TV, and Amazon Fire, TBN's life-changing content is available 24/7 to a world searching for answers.

"God has faithfully answered our prayer to 'ask for the nations,'" said Matt Crouch, "and He has done so above and beyond all that we could ask or think."

Small by today's standards, this little transmitter still put TBN's San José, Costa Rica station on the air.

> The birthplace of Enlace, our all-Spanish Latin American network! With Matt and camera at my side, I am actually holding a ten-watt TV transmitter in my hand—which covered about four square blocks of San José, Costa Rica. Today we cover all of Latin America and all the way to Spain with full-power transmitters and six satellites. ¡Gloria a Dios!
>
> — Paul F. Crouch

The dedication of Enlace's Latin American headquarters.

Paul and Jonas Gonzalez Sr. discussing ways to reach Latin America with the gospel.

Thanking God for new equipment for the Costa Rica station.

Thumbs up for Christian TV in Latin America: Paul with Enlace founder Jonas Gonzalez Sr.

In 1990 Nicaragua's new president, Violeta Chamorro, clearly fell in love with Matt and Laurie's little Caylan. Said Paul Crouch, "I am sure that is why we got a TV station license that same day! Our Enlace channel is on the air in Nicaragua. All glory be to God!"

Over the years Enlace has continued to grow throughout Latin America and the U.S., and is today one of the largest Spanish-language Christian television networks on earth.

Matt and Laurie, along with Joel and Victoria Osteen, met up with Russian rock music icon Stas Namin in Moscow in 2017.

Paul Crouch in Russia in 1990.

"St. Petersburg, Russia: The mayor and officials of St. Petersburg had just given TBN approval for the first Christian TV station in Russia! Jan and I were rejoicing—and where better than under the monument to Lenin, father of atheistic communism! He is gone. TBN TV is on! Praise the Lord!" —Paul F. Crouch

To Russia with Love

For many years Paul and Jan Crouch faithfully prayed to take Christian television behind what was then Russia's Iron Curtain. That door began to open in 1990 with a trip to Leningrad, where the Crouches met with officials about their vision. That meeting led to Paul Crouch and his team returning in May 1991, where over 70,000 heard the gospel at a TBN rally, with most responding to receive Christ!

That step paved the way for TBN's first Russian affiliate network in 1992. Who could have imagined that this would lead to all of Russia, Ukraine, the Baltics, and Eastern Europe being covered by Christian television through TBN?

Though conflict and unrest continue in that troubled region, millions now have the hope and grace found only in Jesus. Remarkably, Matt Crouch was able to interview Mikhail Gorbachev, the final leader of the Soviet Union, before his death in August 2022. Mr. Gorbachev spoke warmly about his unlikely friendship with President Ronald Reagan — and his family's relationship with God.

Ben Miller, TBN's VP of Engineering, checking out the transmitter in St. Petersburg, Russia.

Interviewing Mikhail Gorbachev, final leader of the Soviet Union, as Mr. Gorbachev's Russian translator looks on.

Enjoying our time together with Mikhail Gorbachev!

Both Matt and Laurie had a special opportunity to hug Mikhail Gorbachev. Behind Laurie is a portrait of Mr. Gorbachev's beloved wife, Raisa.

> "With five seasons and over 250 shows under our belt, we have no plans to slow down. Every *Huckabee* episode is an informative, entertaining — and inspiring — adventure. We're just getting started!"
>
> — Mike Huckabee

The Gatlin Brothers perform one of their many hit songs on Huckabee.

Country legend Charlie Daniels.

EDWARD MOSBERG

Edward Mosberg tells his story of surviving the Holocaust.

Gov. Mike with comedian and Hee Haw *star Lulu Roman.*

Roots music acoustic ensemble Appalachian Road Show stirs it up on Huckabee.

Sergey and Sasha perform their breathtaking acrobatics.

Gary "Lt. Dan" Sinise joins Mike to talk about his bestselling book Grateful American.

The Oak Ridge Boys are a Huckabee *fan favorite.*

Stephen and Alex Kendrick sit down with Gov. Mike to talk about their 2019 film Overcomer.

Brian "Head" Welch shares his moving testimony on Huckabee.

"Front Porch" America on TBN

Conservative voice Charlie Kirk, founder of Turning Point USA.

Mike sits down with author, pastor, and leadership coach John Maxwell.

Dennis Prager offers some great observations on the state of American culture.

Comedian Rich Little puts Gov. Mike in stitches.

Former Vice President Mike Pence talks about the hope for America's future.

Iconic rock and country guitarist James Burton performs a classic, with Mike backing on bass.

Gov. Mike with Colorado Congresswoman Lauren Boebert.

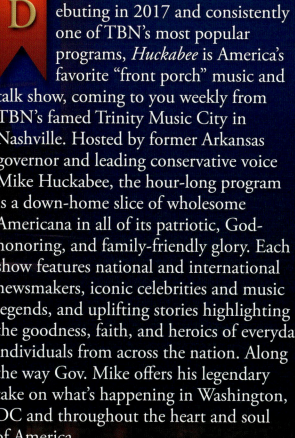

Debuting in 2017 and consistently one of TBN's most popular programs, *Huckabee* is America's favorite "front porch" music and talk show, coming to you weekly from TBN's famed Trinity Music City in Nashville. Hosted by former Arkansas governor and leading conservative voice Mike Huckabee, the hour-long program is a down-home slice of wholesome Americana in all of its patriotic, God-honoring, and family-friendly glory. Each show features national and international newsmakers, iconic celebrities and music legends, and uplifting stories highlighting the goodness, faith, and heroics of everyday individuals from across the nation. Along the way Gov. Mike offers his legendary take on what's happening in Washington, DC and throughout the heart and soul of America.

Celebrity chef Paula Deen cooks up something delicious!

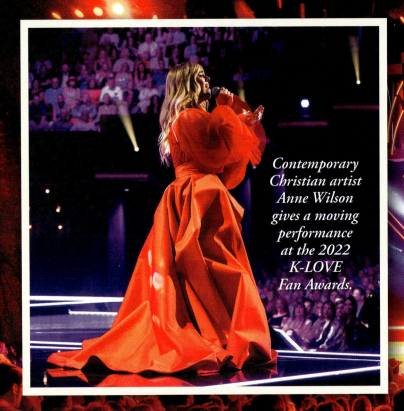

Contemporary Christian artist Anne Wilson gives a moving performance at the 2022 K-LOVE Fan Awards.

2022 K-LOVE Fan Awards: Tauren Wells and Aaron Cole bring the audience to their feet with a rousing duet.

Matthew West joins rapper Lathan Warlick during the TBN special My Story, Your Glory.

Maverick City Music brings passionate worship to the K-LOVE Fan Awards.

Matthew West hosts a TBN worship special.

Grammy- and Dove Award-winning singer-songwriter Michael W. Smith has been a guest on many of TBN's Nashville music and worship specials.

Bill Gaither and the Gaither Vocal Band create some great holiday harmonies for their TBN Christmas Special.

Phil Wickham performs a worship song.

TBN and Nashville — Great Music!

Pastor Mike Jr.

Riley Clemmons

Danny Gokey and Natalie Grant team up for a TBN Christmas special.

Steven Curtis Chapman performs for the TBN Christmas special Let Us Adore Him.

Evvie McKinney

Lauren Daigle and CeCe Winans

Francesca Battistelli

Jekalyn Carr performs for the Gospel Music Association's Let Us Adore Him Christmas special.

We the Kingdom

The combination of Nashville and TBN has always meant the very best in worship, gospel, and contemporary Christian music. For starters, each year TBN serves as the exclusive television broadcaster of Christian music's two top award events, both occurring in Nashville: the GMA Dove Awards and the K-LOVE Fan Awards.

But that's not all. TBN's Nashville studio, known by many as Trinity Music City, regularly hosts the very best that Christian music has to offer, from Grammy and Dove Award winning artists like Michael W. Smith, CeCe Winans, and Jason Crabb, to international favorites like Keith and Kristyn Getty, Southern Gospel legends the Oak Ridge Boys, Bill Gaither and Friends, and many more!

Like father, like son: From the time he was a child, Matt was often on the set as Paul Crouch was busy making films for the Assemblies of God. And as TBN was launched he pitched in, helping to build sets, manning cameras—doing whatever needed to be done to get a program on the air. "If my dad had been a plumber, that's probably what I'd be doing today," said Matt. "Instead, I followed him into filmmaking and Christian television."

Cody Crouch helps dad Matt set up the camera for a scene in the 2010 movie Preacher's Kid.

Paul and Matt confer on a scene during the filming of The Omega Code: *Paul authored the original novel.*

Paul was comfortable on either side of the camera.

Paul on location: "There's nothing quite like being behind a movie camera."

Father and son worked closely to keep the movie as exciting and real as the original book.

Caylan, Cody, Matt, and Laurie at the world premiere.

Actor Ravil Isyanov as Rykoff, the computer expert who cracks the Bible code.

Both *The Omega Code* and its "prequel" *Megiddo: The Omega Code 2* are riveting big-screen thrillers that capture the life-and-death struggle between good and evil while handing viewers a pair of heart-thumping, action-packed stories loaded with intrigue and suspense.

Michael York (center) stars in both The Omega Code *and* Megiddo: The Omega Code 2.

Thumbs up to Megiddo.

World premiere of The Omega Code.

"General" Crouch makes his appearance on the set. Megiddo *is based on Paul's novel of the same title.*

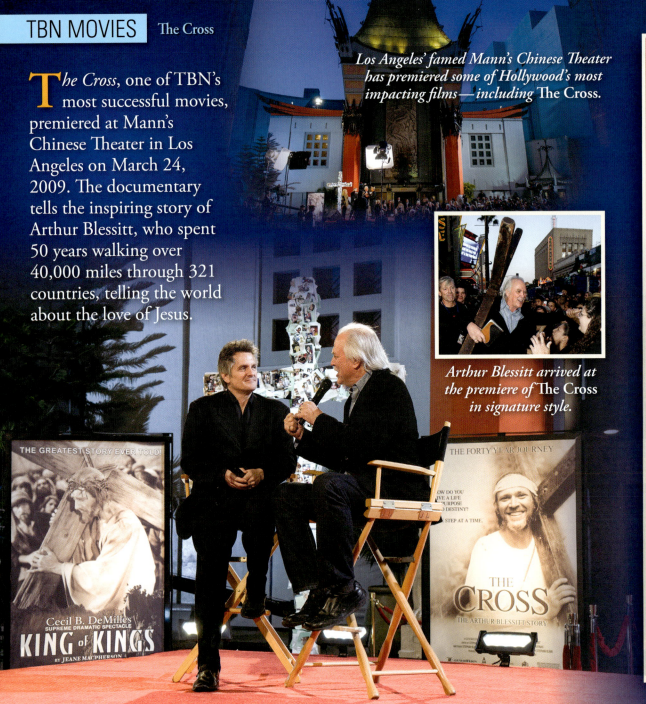

The Cross, one of TBN's most successful movies, premiered at Mann's Chinese Theater in Los Angeles on March 24, 2009. The documentary tells the inspiring story of Arthur Blessitt, who spent 50 years walking over 40,000 miles through 321 countries, telling the world about the love of Jesus.

Los Angeles' famed Mann's Chinese Theater has premiered some of Hollywood's most impacting films—including The Cross.

Arthur Blessitt arrived at the premiere of The Cross *in signature style.*

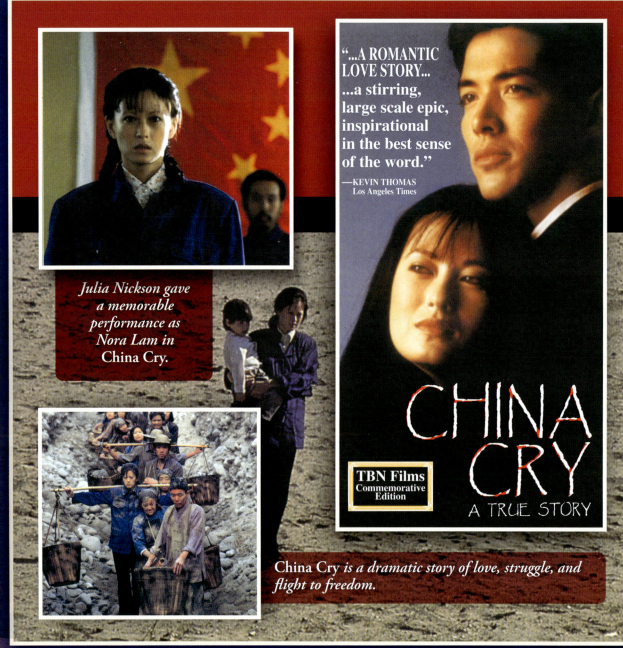

Julia Nickson gave a memorable performance as Nora Lam in China Cry.

"...A ROMANTIC LOVE STORY... ...a stirring, large scale epic, inspirational in the best sense of the word."
—KEVIN THOMAS
Los Angeles Times

CHINA CRY
A TRUE STORY

TBN Films
Commemorative
Edition

China Cry is a dramatic story of love, struggle, and flight to freedom.

One of the most ambitious projects of TBN and Gener8Xion Entertainment, *One Night With the King* is the breathtaking story of Hadassah, the young Jewish girl who through divine intervention becomes Esther, Queen of Persia.

With Tommy Tenney, author of the book Hadassah: One Night With the King.

Luke Goss (right) played King Xerxes in One Night With the King.

Pastors Myles Munroe and A.R. Bernard were guests at the world premiere of One Night With the King.

Singer, actor, and longtime TBN partner Pat Boone at the world premiere.

John Noble played a convincing Admantha, the scheming prince who plots to become king himself.

Actress Tiffany Dupont, who portrayed Queen Esther, with Tommy "Tiny" Lister, who played Hegai in One Night With the King.

China and Beyond

Nora Lam and Paul (below) in the government-approved church in Shanghai, China. The report from TBN's March 1986 newsletter reads as follows: "With Red Guard posted everywhere in the State-owned church, Paul and Nora stood and proclaimed the Good News! Paul was presented as an American 'Success Speaker' and as he stood to speak, Nora said, 'Paul, this is our chance — GO FOR IT!' Paul preached and prayed the sinner's prayer, and at the end the entire congregation gave them a standing ovation and many gave their lives to Jesus!"

"In 1979 a group of TBN partners accompanied Jan and me on a trip to mainland China. When we saw this sign at the border we stopped, and as I poured Holy Land anointing oil over it we claimed China for Jesus." - Paul

CHINA BELONGS TO GOD!

"It was forbidden, but we did it anyway! Yes, Nora Lam translated my sermon into Mandarin Chinese. Secret police watched and listened nervously at the Shanghai Three-Self Church as Carolyn Sundseth and other members of the Reagan White House staff backed me up! Fifty percent of those who attended stood to pray the sinner's prayer. The rest gave a standing ovation. Today, the gospel goes into China by satellite, cable, and the Internet 24/7! Praise the Lord!"
— Paul F. Crouch

Meeting with Chinese television executives in Beijing.

With Joel and Victoria Osteen on the Great Wall of China in 2017.

While mainland China remains closed, untold millions of individuals there are hungry to know more about Jesus. Some access TBN through VPN technology, while others can occasionally view Christian programming on Taiwanese networks like Good TV and BSTV. Said Matt Crouch: "We continue to pray that God will open doors for TBN to share the good news of Jesus throughout China."

IRAQ — HERE WE COME!
I WILL DO A NEW THING!

" O n Mount Nebo in Jordan, I got to see what Moses saw as the children of Israel prepared to cross the Jordan into the Promised Land. Moses did not get to go, but saw the land from this mount. He was buried by God somewhere near this site. **—** Paul F. Crouch **"**

"REMEMBER YE NOT THE FORMER THINGS...BEHOLD, I WILL DO A NEW THING; NOW IT SHALL SPRING FORTH; SHALL YE NOT KNOW IT?" ISA. 43:18, 19

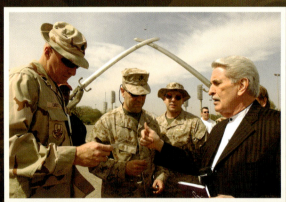

Meeting with U.S. troops during a trip to Iraq in 2004.

Amman, Jordan

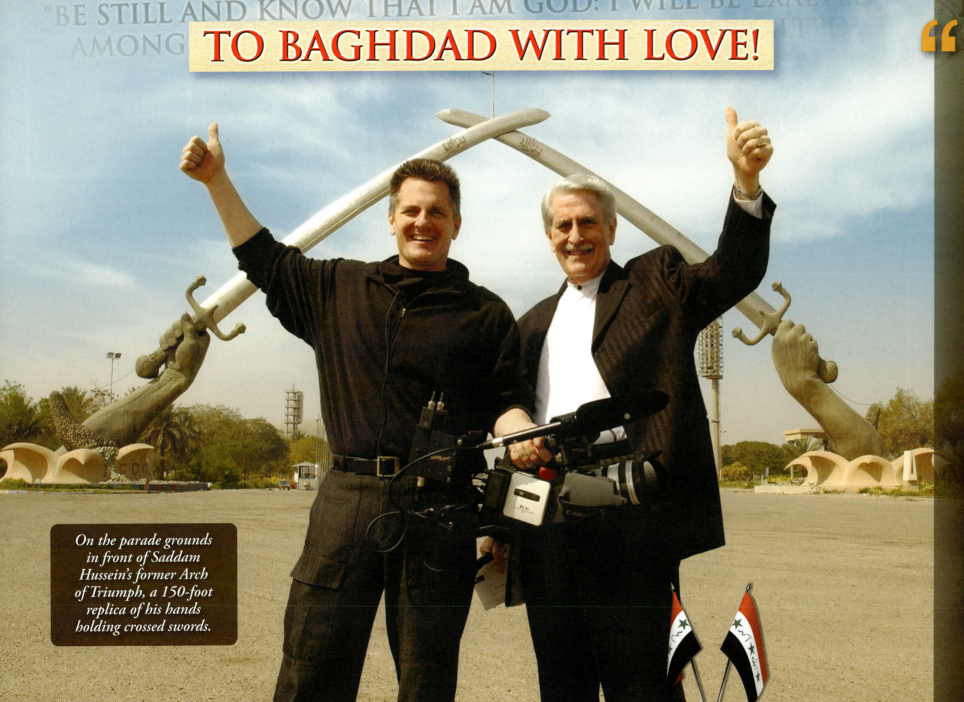

TO BAGHDAD WITH LOVE!

"BE STILL AND KNOW THAT I AM GOD: I WILL BE EXALTED AMONG

On the parade grounds in front of Saddam Hussein's former Arch of Triumph, a 150-foot replica of his hands holding crossed swords.

"In 2004 I made what was possibly the most historic missionary journey in the 40-year history of TBN. It would take a thousand pages to tell of all the miracles God did in Jordan and Iraq in the space of about three days. I honestly believe that Matt and I, with our small group, were made invisible to the barriers, checkpoints, armed guards, military infrastructure, and enemies all around us! Supernatural favor was our portion as we moved effortlessly through the war-torn and suffering city of Baghdad."
— Paul F. Crouch

Paul purchased a satellite dish from a vendor in downtown Baghdad and gave it to a local church.

TBN's *Praise* program has featured many outstanding guests whose lives and ministries have touched millions of viewers.

Rhonda Fleming Carlson

Dr. Creflo Dollar

Pastor Erwin McManus

CeCe and Delores "Mom" Winans

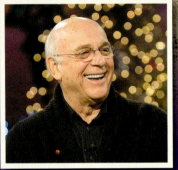

Gavin MacLeod

Faith-and-family movie producer David A.R. White.

Comedian Steve Harvey with singer Donnie McClurkin.

Dean and Mary Brown enjoy a light moment with Calvary Chapel founder Chuck Smith.

Host Phil Munsey welcomed ministry couples Joel and Victoria Osteen (left) and Joseph and Wendy Prince.

Doctors Frederick and Betty Price

Max Lucado

Matt and Laurie hosting *Praise* from West Angeles Church of God in Christ. Guests: Johnny Wright, Brian Littrell, Pastor Tommy Tenney.

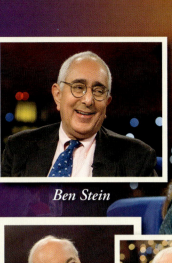

Ben Stein

Comedian Tim Conway with his dog Leo.

Mr. T has been a frequent guest on Praise, *but this was the first time "I pity the fool" was uttered on Christian television.*

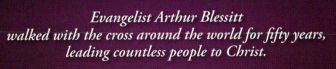

Evangelist Arthur Blessitt walked with the cross around the world for fifty years, leading countless people to Christ.

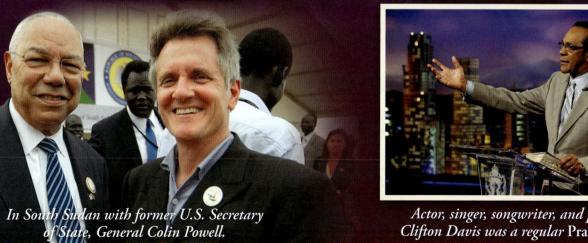

In South Sudan with former U.S. Secretary of State, General Colin Powell.

Actor, singer, songwriter, and pastor Clifton Davis was a regular Praise *host.*

World-renowned preachers, teachers, musicians, artists, athletes, and many others appear on TBN's *Praise* program.

World evangelism was the focus as Matt and Paul (center) welcomed Mark Anderson of Call2All; Loren Cunningham, founder of Youth With a Mission; and Steve Douglas and Brad Bright of Campus Crusade for Christ.

Author, speaker, and pastor John Maxwell explained some important leadership concepts.

Vietnam veteran and evangelist Dave Roever has been a longtime friend of TBN.

Former New York Mets and Yankees slugger Darryl Strawberry and his wife Tracy appeared on Praise from New York City. Phil Munsey was the host.

Dave Stotts hosts the popular TBN series Drive Thru History.

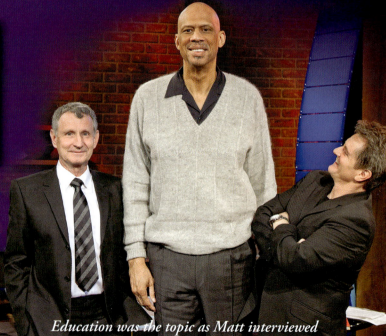

At Dodger Stadium with Joel and Victoria Osteen for the 2012 Night of Hope celebration.

Education was the topic as Matt interviewed Professor Raymond Obstfeld, along with NBA Hall of Famer and STEM (Science, Technology, Engineering and Math) advocate Kareem Abdul-Jabbar.

Andraé Crouch

Ken and Joni Eareckson Tada

John Schneider

Brian "Head" Welch

Natalie Cole

Sinbad

Chuck and Gena Norris

Richard Twiss

Jim Caviezel played Jesus in The Passion of the Christ.

Kim Alexis

Leon Patillo

In Times Square, New York City, with Pastors Phil Munsey and Joel Osteen.

Two-time World Heavyweight Champion George Foreman.

T.D. Jakes shares a word from Scripture.

Crouch Family at Taj Mahal, in India

From one small station broadcasting a few hours of snowy, homemade Christian programming each night, to a family of 30 (and growing) global networks sending out life-changing television 24/7 to every corner of the earth — well, it's nothing short of a miracle! "We knew God had something big in mind when we signed on the air back in 1973," recalled Paul Crouch. "We just didn't know how big. And we've only just begun!"

The TBN team in Prague, the capital city of the Czech Republic.

"TBN-Asia in Manila, Philippines serves as the satellite hub for all of TBN's outreach across the continent of Asia. As you can see, this enormous responsibility is in some good hands. We are thankful for the many individuals throughout the world who work diligently to make sure the life-changing programming of TBN is flowing around the clock.
— Paul F. Crouch"

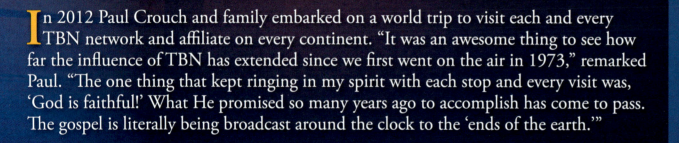

Stephan Karl Gaatz and Beate Busch of Germany's Bibel TV, a member of the TBN Family of Networks.

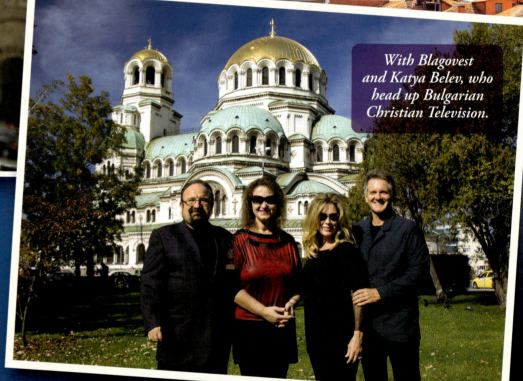

With Blagovest and Katya Belev, who head up Bulgarian Christian Television.

In 2012 Paul Crouch and family embarked on a world trip to visit each and every TBN network and affiliate on every continent. "It was an awesome thing to see how far the influence of TBN has extended since we first went on the air in 1973," remarked Paul. "The one thing that kept ringing in my spirit with each stop and every visit was, 'God is faithful!' What He promised so many years ago to accomplish has come to pass. The gospel is literally being broadcast around the clock to the 'ends of the earth.'"

With Enlace staff member, Melissa, at TBN's station in Bogotá, Colombia.

F rom Europe to Africa, and all through the continent of Asia, TBN's programming is touching millions with the gospel and challenging believers to go deeper in their faith.

Meeting with Pastor Blagovest Belev of Bulgarian Christian Television.

TBN's managers from around the world pictured with Paul, Matt, and Laurie in front of the Duomo di Milano in Milan, Italy.

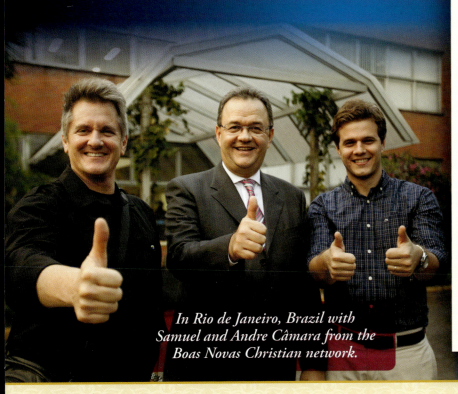

In Rio de Janeiro, Brazil with Samuel and Andre Câmara from the Boas Novas Christian network.

From over-the-air, cable, and satellite broadcast to online and social media platforms, TBN's broad range of faith-and-family programming is available to more individuals than ever across the earth. "Our vision for TBN today and in the coming years," said Matt Crouch, "is to flood every broadcast and digital platform with relevant, life-changing content so that individuals everywhere have access to the good news of Jesus any time, anywhere, and on any electronic device."

Paul and Matt on a train traveling through China in 2012. "TBN came in crystal clear on our smart phones and iPads," said Matt.

On location in Dubai (left): The advance of technology has made many of TBN's global networks available throughout the world.

In Istanbul, Turkey with Pastor Reza Safa of Nejat TV.

With the staff of TBN Polska, our affiliate network reaching all of Poland.

It's "thumbs up" from Helsinki, Finland with Hannu Haukka of Alfa TV.

Preparing to tape a special program in Prague, Czech Republic.

Visiting the JCTV Pakistan staff and studios in the city of Lahore.

Meeting of TBN's European affiliate managers in Prague.

Passing the Torch

During the final meeting of TBN's memorable Holy Land tour in September 2012, Paul Crouch passed the mantle of leadership he and Jan had carried for nearly forty years on to Matt and Laurie Crouch. How this unique anointed moment came to happen is a remarkable story worth telling.

TBN ministry partner Joseph Prince was the special teacher and guest host for the tour, and he recalled that on the evening before he was to preach at the last session of the tour at Caesarea Maritima, he was having dinner with Matt, Laurie, their two sons Caylan and Cody, Paul Crouch, and Samuel Smadja, an Israeli Christian and good friend of TBN.

Recalled Joseph of that evening: "During the dinner, the Lord gave me an inward vision of Dr. Paul laying hands on his son Matt. Those who are familiar with my ministry know that I am not given to offering a lot of prophetic words. And that is why I re-

> "I believe that in the years to come, the name of Jesus ... will be lifted up and exalted like never before through TBN."
>
> – Joseph Prince

member saying to Dr. Paul, 'I hope that I am not stepping out of line by asking this, but have you laid hands on Matt publicly?' Dr. Paul shared with me that he had laid his hands on Matt privately when they were back home, but had not done so publicly yet.

"And that was when Dr. Paul opened up his Bible and shared with us from Hebrews chapter 12, relating how the Lord had already spoken to him regarding Matt and the future of TBN. At the top of that page in his Bible, Dr. Paul showed me that he had written the words, 'Run, Matt, Run!'

"Wow! I had no idea! I was simply being obedient to the Lord, faithfully reporting the vision that He had given me. It turned out to be a confirmation of what the Lord had put on Dr. Paul's heart. One thing led to another, and before we left the dinner table, Dr. Paul asked if I could pray over Matt as he transferred the mantle of TBN's leadership to Matt and Laurie at Caesarea Maritima.

In Caesarea Paul laid hands on Matt and Laurie, passing to them the TBN leadership anointing that he and Jan carried over the past forty years.

"The very next day, as we stood before a live audience of some 2,000 people in the ancient amphitheater where the Apostle Paul preached the gospel of grace to King Agrippa, Dr. Paul laid his hands on Matt and Laurie, and together we prayed over them.

"I am awed and humbled that the Lord and Dr. Paul gave me the opportunity to be a part of such a momentous occasion that not only impacts Christian television, but also Christendom as a whole. It is remarkable that this historic event took place as TBN was approaching its fortieth anniversary. Forty years in the Bible is highly significant as it speaks of a generation. David ruled as king for forty years before Solomon his son ascended the throne. Furthermore, the transfer of the mantle of TBN's leadership occurred in Caesarea Maritima —the very place where the Apostle Paul launched forth to proclaim the gospel of grace.

"It is beyond any doubt that this was a divinely orchestrated event. God is appointing a new generation to build upon the legacy of TBN and, in these last days, to launch forth to proclaim the gospel of grace throughout the world with boldness and authority."

Pastor Prince concluded with this powerful thought: "I believe that in the years to come, the name of Jesus, the power of His finished work, and the glorious gospel of grace will be lifted up and exalted like never before through TBN. You ain't seen nothing yet, Matt! The best is yet to come! As Dr. Paul wrote, 'Run, Matt, Run!'"

"Run Matt, Run!"

Paul, Matt, and Laurie on **Behind the Scenes** *from TBN's Jerusalem studio.*

"That was the word of the Lord that flooded my spirit as I prayed about the future of TBN! Knowing that soon Jan and I would be compelled to pass the torch, it was clear to us both that our son Matthew and his wife, Laurie, were chosen by God for the challenge ahead. The scripture that leaped from the page was prophetic:

'... let us run with patience the race that is set before us, looking unto Jesus, the author and finisher of our faith ....'
–Hebrews 12:1-2, KJV

Two generations of leadership: Just as Paul and Jan partnered together for forty years in leading the miracle of TBN, Matt and Laurie have committed to walk hand-in-hand, co-laboring as faithful stewards to continue and expand TBN's global impact.

"The other word was 'CHALLENGE,' as I had the joy of pouring into their hearts the spiritual meaning of that word. Challenge is, in effect, trusting God for victory as you face the enemy at each new conquest for the Kingdom. Some of these challenges are so forbidding they seem impossible, and like the prophet Jeremiah you are tempted to give up and quit. Yet, when you are called of God you will say with Jeremiah:

'... His word was in my heart like a burning fire shut up in my bones; I was weary of holding it back, and I could not.' – Jeremiah 20:9

"It was a glorious experience in the land of Israel to hand the spiritual torch to my children and say to them, 'Run Matt and Laurie, Run!'

Paul

TBN
NETWORKS

Russell Hall, TBN's senior vice president of production, directs a program for distribution across multiple global broadcast platforms.

> "Our mission is to capture the hearts of this generation through compelling content that clearly communicates the message of God's hope and grace."
> — Matt Crouch

Together we're reaching every nation and people with the life-transforming message of the gospel.

New TBN Poland facilities

New TBN South Africa studios

New TBN studio in Italy

New hotel and TBN studio in Israel

New production facilities in Dallas

Expanding Our Global Reach and Impact

... through strategically located production facilities

REACHING HUNDREDS OF MILLIONS VIA OVER-THE-AIR CABLE / SATELLITE & ONLINE PLATFORMS

Matt and Laurie in the construction zone of TBN's new Dallas production facility.

Every Nation & Generation

When Paul and Jan Crouch launched TBN in 1973, their goal was to give people everywhere access to life-changing Christian television. That meant establishing TV stations wherever God opened the doors. They represented what we might call the "hardware generation," painstakingly building stations and studios, towers and transmitters with brick, mortar, cement, and steel — beginning in the U.S. and ultimately spreading TBN's broadcast footprint across the earth.

Fast-forward fifty years, and through cable, satellite, and over-the-air broadcast, TBN is now available twenty-four hours a day in over 178 nations and seventeen languages. Add to that the explosion of digital viewing platforms over the Internet, and it's no stretch to say that millions of individuals around the world have access to TBN's programming.

Although the call for new towers, transmitters, and brick-and-mortar stations has mostly disappeared, there is now a desperate need for something else: a steady supply of powerful and impacting programming that will draw in those millions of potential viewers across the earth, telling and showing them the good news of Jesus Christ in a relevant manner.

"While my parents were the hardware generation, we are the 'software generation,'" said Matt Crouch. "Their mission was to pioneer and build the infrastructure of Christian television. Our mission is to capture the hearts of this generation through compelling content that clearly communicates the message of God's hope and grace."

The great news is that through the development of state-of-the-art production studios in strategic locales like Poland, South Africa, Italy, Israel, the U.S., and elsewhere, TBN can flood the earth with programming and content that will draw millions to Christ.

"I believe we're on the leading edge of a major Kingdom harvest in the days ahead," said Matt. "And as my father said many times, our passion and purpose at TBN is all about 'souls, souls, souls.'"

> TBN is positioned to flood the earth with programming and content that will draw millions to Christ.

Compelling, Original TBN Content!

THE JOURNEY
A MUSIC SPECIAL FROM
ANDREA BOCELLI

There's no question that the landscape of Christian television has changed dramatically over the past few years, and TBN has been at the forefront of the transformation. While teaching and ministry programs continue to be important to many viewers, TBN has taken the lead in introducing an exciting new era of content that breaks the mold of traditional Christian programming.

From current events and talk shows, to documentaries, music, and more, TBN is drawing new viewer demographics from across the earth through content that is entertaining, informative, inspirational —and life-changing.

Check out a sampling on these pages of TBN's innovative new content that is changing the face of Christian programming.

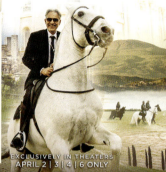

Matt with world-renowned tenor Andrea Bocelli and wife Veronica Berti Bocelli during filming of The Journey.

Theatrical poster for The Journey.

Andrea Bocelli with a priest near St. Peter's Basilica.

Performance at the Abbey of San Galgano in Tuscany.

The Journey premieres in NYC's Times Square.

Andrea Bocelli during the filming of a performance with French soprano Clara Barbier Serrano.

THE STORY BEHIND THE STORY
with Mike Rowe

ROUTE 60
THE BIBLICAL HIGHWAY
FOLLOW AN ANCIENT ROAD TO A BRIGHTER FUTURE
IN THEATERS STARTING SEPTEMBER 18TH
AMBASSADOR DAVID FRIEDMAN   SECRETARY MIKE POMPEO

THE ABRAHAM ACCORDS

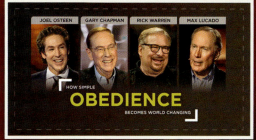

JOEL OSTEEN   GARY CHAPMAN   RICK WARREN   MAX LUCADO
HOW SIMPLE
OBEDIENCE
BECOMES WORLD CHANGING

CODY CROUCH PRESENTS
This Month in Christian History

MYSTERIES OF THE MESSIAH
WITH RABBI JASON SOBEL

GAITHER
A LEGACY IN MUSIC

HUCKABEE

THE ROSENBERG REPORT

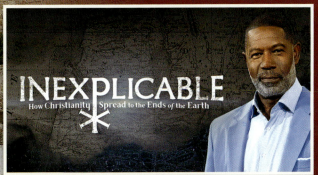

INEXPLICABLE
How Christianity Spread to the Ends of the Earth

Better TOGETHER

Bishop T.D. Jakes teaching in one of the episodes of the original TBN series Crushing: God Turns Pressure into Power.

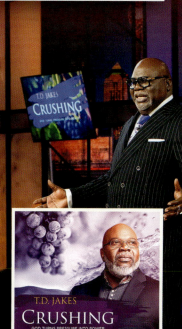

T.D. JAKES
CRUSHING
GOD TURNS PRESSURE INTO POWER

TV for Everyone!

One important thing we've learned in TBN's fifty years (and counting) on the air is the importance of variety. That's why we've been steadily expanding our network lineup — to offer quality, cutting-edge programming and content that appeals to a wide variety of viewers. We call it "TV for everyone," and here are a few of the TBN channels reaching viewers with focused content:

SMILE offers a round-the-clock lineup of entertaining, educational, and totally wholesome programming for children ages 2-12.

Positv brings viewers a 24/7 supply of quality movies filled with messages of hope, encouragement, triumph, and redemption.

TBN Select brings you an online selection of trending programming from TBN's most-watched networks around the world.

Add to that our many digital channels offering bite-sized content from across TBN's global platforms, and you've got a treasure of cutting-edge content for every viewer demographic.

iShine KNECT inspires and entertains 8- to 13-year-old "tween" viewers.

"There's nothing more satisfying than bringing a broad range of high-quality, engaging content to as many viewers across the earth as possible. That has become the next-generation vision for all we do at TBN."

— Matt Crouch

Positiv TV brings you quality movies filled with messages of hope, encouragement, triumph, and redemption.

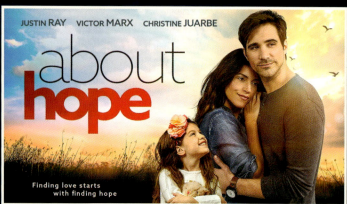

Fun and Faith-Filled Viewing Just for Kids!

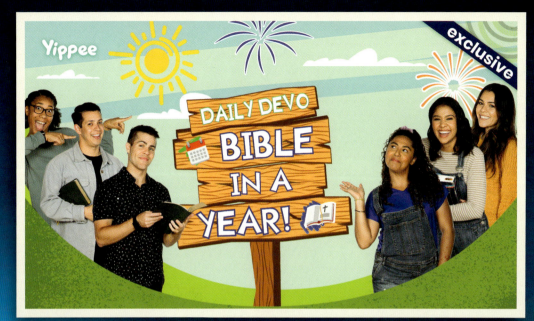

exclusive

Yippee

DAILY DEVO
BIBLE IN A YEAR!

Yippee.tv

FACE YOUR FEARS WITH THE MOORES

BackSeat DRIVERS

MAGGIE'S MARKET

New VeggieTales

Watch *VeggieTales* at Yippee.tv

YIPPEE IS THE WORLD'S LARGEST FAITH-BASED
STREAMING SERVICE FOR CHILDREN

SCAN TO LEARN MORE

More than ever, children need a safe place where they can enjoy wholesome programming made for them. That's why TBN launched Yippee, the totally secure streaming service parents trust for their kids. Yippee is filled with thousands of hours of entertaining, educational, and inspirational content that reinforces the values parents and grandparents want for their little ones.

Since its 2020 launch Yippee has become the world's largest faith-based streaming service for children. Best of all, Yippee features exclusive and original faith-filled content, including the world's first car show for kids, *Backseat Drivers*, plus kid-friendly favorites like *Face Your Fears With the Moores*, the *Daily Devo* show, *Maggie's Market*, and of course, *VeggieTales*, including all new programs and the most extensive collection of episodes anywhere.

Check out Yippee for yourself at Yippee.tv.

The VeggieTales SHOW

Christmas is a joyous celebration as Bob, Larry, and the VeggieTales gang find memorable and entertaining ways to share the story of Jesus' birth with children and families.

"Moms and dads have always appreciated how *VeggieTales* entertains kids while gently pointing them to Jesus. And that continues to be a priority with these fresh, new episodes of *The VeggieTales Show*."

— Matt Crouch

Matt and Laurie welcome Bob the Tomato and Larry the Cucumber to talk about their exclusive TBN program, The VeggieTales Show.

A New Chapter for VeggieTales

For thirty years and counting, Bob the Tomato, Larry the Cucumber, and the rest of the *Veggie Tales* gang have been reaching children with unforgettable Bible stories, award-winning animation, and entertaining "silly songs," all while teaching them important life values like kindness, compassion, honesty—and faith in God.

And for more than a few of those years moms and dads who grew up with this zany crew of cartoon vegetables have been sitting down with their own kids to enjoy *Veggie Tales* on TBN.

Now TBN has teamed up with *Veggie Tales* creators Phil Vischer, Mike Nawrocki, and the Big Idea Content Group for an all-new version of everyone's favorite vegetable ensemble, called *The VeggieTales Show*.

Through that partnership TBN has introduced 26 exciting episodes of *The Veggie Tales Show*, with each half-hour show featuring everyone's favorite *Veggie Tales* characters performing all-new Bible stories, singing new silly songs, and doing the crazy stunts that made classic *Veggie Tales* such a family favorite.

"Moms and dads have always appreciated how *Veggie Tales* entertains kids while gently pointing them to Jesus," said Matt Crouch. "And that continues to be a priority with these new episodes of *The VeggieTales Show.*"

He noted that millions of children have been impacted by the values they've learned through watching *Veggie Tales* on TBN. "Now we're thrilled to be producing a new era of *Veggie Tales* that will reach kids for many years to come," said Matt. "It's this investment in quality programming for younger generations that really matters."

He added that "*Veggie Tales* has always been a perfect fit for TBN, and that's why we're so excited about this partnership. We believe that the truths kids are going to experience through these entertaining and hilarious new *Veggie Tales* episodes will impact them for a lifetime."

> "... we're thrilled to be producing a new era of *VeggieTales* that will reach kids for many years to come."
> – Matt Crouch

VeggieTales animator.

26 NEW EPISODES

All 26 new VeggieTales episodes available exclusively at

Yippee.tv

SCAN TO LEARN MORE

Cartoon stars Bob the Tomato and Larry the Cucumber (center) with a few of the VeggieTales gang.

Inspirational Content On Demand

The landscape of broadcast television has changed drastically in the fifty years since TBN first took to the airwaves. Back in 1973, if you wanted to view Christian programming, you switched on your living room set and watched whatever happened to be playing at the moment.

Not so today. Video on Demand (VOD) gives you thousands of hours of the best in TBN programming at your fingertips whenever and wherever you want to view it. From your favorite episode of *Praise*, *Huckabee*, *Better Together*, and other originals, to TBN's most popular pastors and teachers like David Jeremiah, Robert Morris, Joel Osteen, and many others, with TBN's VOD platform you're in the driver's seat for the life-changing programming you want to view or share with someone else.

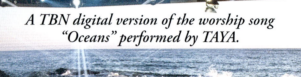

A TBN digital version of the worship song "Oceans" performed by TAYA.

Behind the Scenes: TBN's compelling content is produced in state-of-the-art production facilities around the world.

TBN programming is available anytime and anywhere on smart phones, tablets, and other electronic devices.

Search Results for "Praise" "2022" "2023"

S50:E50

Praise - Shawn Bolz - August 25, 2022

S1:E559

Praise - Joyce Meyer - January 3, 2023

S1:E572

Praise - Lysa TerKeurst - April 27, 2023

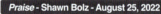

TBN's Digital Platforms Reaching Millions!

> "The expansion of online platforms across the earth means that anyone with a smart phone, tablet, or other electronic device has access to life-changing TBN content anytime, anywhere. — Matt Crouch"

DOWNLOAD THE TBN APP TO YOUR FAVORITE DEVICE

 tv iPhone iPad firetv Roku android androidtv

From smart phones to iPads, tablets, and other devices, viewers across the earth are consuming billions of hours of content every day on online apps and social media sites. And in their searching, millions are discovering TBN's message of hope through Christ.

In fact, every year TBN's YouTube channels alone garner hundreds of millions of views from individuals who are drawn to short clips from such TBN programs as *Praise, Huckabee, Better Together,* and *Centerpoint.*

Each one of those views are of TBN content selected to draw individuals to the love of Jesus. The truly great news is that many of TBN's digital viewers are responding, calling our TBN prayer line, finding answers to their needs — and experiencing new life in Christ.

THE RAMSEY SHOW

Jesus IN THE PASSOVER

STATE of FAITH

JOEL + VICTORIA YANKEE STADIUM

K-LOVE Fan Awards

Tauren Wells and Matthew West hosted the 2022 K-LOVE Fan Awards.

The only fan-voted awards program for Christian music and media, the K-LOVE Fan Awards has been airing exclusively on TBN since 2018. Each year K-LOVE brings together the biggest names in Christian music, film, sports, books, and more, celebrating artists, athletes, authors, and entertainers who seek to impact today's culture for Jesus Christ. And TBN is right in the middle of it all, bringing viewers all the excitement the event has to offer.

"TBN is committed to sharing the very best of music and ministry with our global viewing audience," said Matt Crouch. "And our partnership with the K-LOVE Fan Awards is front-and-center in that effort."

TobyMac

Chris Tomlin

Anne Wilson

Michael W. Smith

Joel and Luke Smallbone of FOR KING + COUNTRY.

Katy Nichole (right) won the K-LOVE 2022 Worship Song of the Year award for "In Jesus' Name."

GMA Dove Awards

Jekalyn Carr (left) performs at the Dove Awards.

CeCe Winans won several awards at the 2022 Doves.

Zach Williams

Members of Elevation Worship are interviewed on the red carpet at the GMA Dove Awards.

Phil Wickham

TobyMac performs at the Dove Awards.

For many years TBN has been the television home for the Gospel Music Association's prestigious Dove Awards, the gold standard for singers, songwriters, and Christian music professionals. From Christian music legends to up-and-coming artists, the GMA Dove Awards is the one night of music no one wants to miss.

"Many of the artists recognized and honored with GMA Dove Awards have shared their music and its life-changing message with our viewers on TBN," noted Matt Crouch. "And each year we're excited to share with our global audience the incredible evening honoring those who create the music that brings hope and changes lives."

A Bocelli Family Christmas

CeCe Winans performs for her TBN music special Believe for It.

Andrea Bocelli (left) during filming of the TBN theatrical release The Journey. Michael W. Smith (background) performs in the film.

Joining gospel music legend Bill Gaither and his wife Gloria for the TBN special Gaither: A Legacy in Music.

Jordan St. Cyr sings for *Unsung Hero: A Mother's Day Special.*

Leanna Crawford

Contemporary Christian artist Rebecca St. James with her mother, author Helen Smallbone.

Cody Carnes

Michael W. Smith hosted the TBN worship special Surrounded.

Michael W. Smith

Joel Smallbone of FOR KING + COUNTRY and his wife Moriah are interviewed during the 2022 K-LOVE Fan Awards.

Exclusive Music Specials

We've teamed up with a number of music legends to produce some truly memorable TBN specials. That includes world-renowned Italian tenor Andrea Bocelli, who has partnered with TBN for several breathtakingly beautiful Christmas productions, along with the theatrical release *The Journey*, which follows Andrea across the Italian countryside on an unforgettable spiritual — and musical — pilgrimage.

In recent years TBN has also produced and aired specials with such award-winning Christian singers, songwriters, and worship leaders as CeCe Winans, Michael W. Smith, Chris Tomlin, and Jason Crabb.

"Music has a way of touching and moving people in a way that nothing else can," noted Matt Crouch. "We've been blessed to partner with true musical legends for some memorable specials TBN viewers continue asking us to air."

Health & Wholeness God's Way!

Viewers have always had an enthusiasm for TBN programming that shows them how to enjoy the healthy lifestyle God created for them. In the 1980s and 1990s viewers tuned in weekly for *Calling Dr. Whitaker*, an early TBN health program with host Dr. Donald Whitaker, a prominent physician who combined God's Word with up-to-date research on nutrition, health, and wholeness.

Today TBN continues to host knowledgeable and experienced experts in health and nutrition like Dr. Scott Hannen, a chiropractic physician and bestselling author of *Healing by Design* and *Stop the Pain*.

One of TBN's most popular guests in the area of health and nutrition is biblical health coach Jordan Rubin, whose *New York Times* bestseller, *The Maker's Diet*, recounts his own dramatic journey from debilitating illness to vibrant health through following the counsel of Scripture.

Jordan and fellow health and nutrition expert, chiropractic physician Dr. Josh Axe, regularly sit down with Matt and Laurie to lay out simple strategies TBN viewers can follow to step into vibrant health and vitality.

> **"We're thrilled to partner with TBN to help people around the world live the healthy lifestyle God intended for them.**
> — Biblical Health Coach Jordan Rubin **"**

Jordan Rubin and Dr. Josh Axe talk health and wellness with TBN viewers.

Dr. Scott Hannen discusses exciting breakthroughs in living healthy and pain-free.

TBN ISRAEL — A Voice in the Holy Land

For fifty years TBN has had a deep love for Israel. Paul and Jan Crouch took seriously God's promise to bless those who bless Israel, and over the years they accompanied thousands of TBN partners to the Holy Land to do just that.

One of Paul's dreams was to establish a broadcast presence in Israel that would bless God's people while sending out the love of Jesus. That dream took shape in 2012 when TBN purchased a beautiful building for a production facility right in the heart of Jerusalem. Matt Crouch explained that unlike most property in Israel, which is owned by the government and leased to groups, TBN's facility— a stone's throw from historic Mount Zion, Mount Moriah, and the Mount of Olives—is owned by the network with no strings attached.

"TBN's state-of-the-art Jerusalem studio rests on a mount called *Givat Hananiah*, which in Hebrew means the 'Hill of Grace,'" Matt said. "The word 'grace' is key here, because from this 'Hill of Grace' TBN is sending the message of God's grace to the world."

In Jerusalem with Joel and Victoria Osteen and Joseph Prince.

On location in Israel: Joel Rosenberg (left) tapes an episode of The Rosenberg Report. *Joseph Prince and Matt Crouch during filming of the series* Expedition Promised Land.

With Sheila Walsh during her first trip to Israel.

Interviewing Israeli Prime Minister Benjamin Netanyahu.

> **I**t's a joy to bring TBN viewers with us to Israel through the programs created by our production team in Jerusalem.
> — Laurie Crouch

With Messianic Rabbi Jason Sobel.

Yael Eckstein (left) with Sheila Walsh and Laurie Crouch during taping of a TBN special in Israel.

On location in Jerusalem during the filming of TBN's The Watchman With Erick Stakelbeck.

Preparing for TBN's 2023 Holy Land tour with Rabbi Jason Sobel and Pastor Jentezen Franklin.

With Pastor Robert Jeffress in Israel.

Matt and archaeologist Shimon Gibson stand at the wall of the old city of Jerusalem.

Pastor Joseph Prince opens Scripture during his TBN series Expedition Promised Land. *(Right) Matt with Joseph during filming.*

Rendering of the new TBN hotel and studio overlooking the Sea of Galilee.

DAVID'S HARP
HOTEL | GALILEE

"TBN's new David's Harp Hotel stands ready to bless both tour groups and the nation of Israel in Capernaum, Jesus' chosen hometown from which he changed the world forever!"

— Matt Crouch

Al Horreya TV

ANOTHER NETWORK IS BORN!

I n 2004 God began opening a significant window for a television network that would broadcast the message of salvation through Jesus Christ to the Arabic-speaking peoples in the Middle East, as well as to the multiplied millions living in the U.S., Europe, and elsewhere.

With its launch the next year, the Healing Channel—now called Al Horreya TV (Arabic for "freedom")—began beaming life-changing programming in the Arabic language around the world, with a particular focus on reaching those in Arabic-speaking nations in the Middle East and Africa.

"While many Muslims are antagonistic toward Christianity," said Paul Crouch, "God has prepared the hearts of millions of precious people in these countries to receive the gospel, and many are coming to Christ everyday through Al Horreya TV."

Paul Crouch (right) discusses the Middle East with Dr. Raafat Girgis from Al Horreya TV.

Paul Crouch's father, Andrew Crouch, was a faithful missionary in Egypt, and Paul himself lived in Egypt as a child.

The Crouch family with Al Horreya TV's Dr. Raafat Girgis.

TO IRAN WITH LOVE

Nejat TV

Pastor Reza Safa of TBN's Nejat TV discusses the need for gospel outreach in Iran.

Nejat TV reaches Farsi-speaking people in Iran, the Middle East, and around the world.

A second TBN network began shining the light of God's love into the Middle East when the Farsi language Nejat TV started broadcasting into Iran and the surrounding areas in 2006. It all began when God spoke to Iranian-American Pastor Reza Safa about taking Jesus to the millions of Muslims in his native country. "Even as Iran and other countries in the Middle East are becoming an increasing threat to Israel and the West, TBN Nejat TV is bringing the message of God's love," Pastor Safa noted. "We are seeing many Muslims abandoning Islam for faith in Christ."

Said Paul Crouch: "Nejat represents TBN's mission to take the gospel to every corner of the earth. God is clear in His Word that perseverance is key to success in His kingdom. The Middle East has been a tough road for the gospel. But as we have persevered in the midst of trial and testing, God has brought success. Nejat represents just one testimony of His faithfulness."

JCTV Pakistan

The good news of Jesus is reaching Pakistan, the Middle East, Asia, and beyond through TBN's JCTV Pakistan affiliate network. What began humbly in 2004 as a local cable television outreach to a small area of the capital city of Lahore, now reaches well over 200 million potential viewers in the Urdu and Hindi languages.

While opposition has been heavy in this Muslim nation, JCTV's dedicated team has pressed on to take Christian television to more cities and regions.

"I strongly believe when the Holy Spirit tells you to go and preach, no hurdles and obstacles can stand before you," said JCTV founder Javed Rauf.

In 2013 JCTV's broadcast reach was increased dramatically when TBN stepped in to place the network on the powerful ABS-2 satellite. Through its partnership with TBN, JCTV now covers all of Pakistan, the entire Indian sub-continent, and even parts of Africa and Europe with the life-changing message of God's love.

In spite of persecution and opposition, JCTV's dedicated staff joyfully broadcasts the message of God's love.

Since 2004 over 125,000 individuals have come to Christ through JCTV Pakistan.

Kanal Hayat

The TBN team in front of the ancient Hagia Sophia cathedral in Istanbul, Turkey.

Turkish-speaking pastors and Christians provide rich, culturally relevant programming.

More than 137 million Turkish-speaking people throughout the Middle East have access to the gospel through Kanal Hayat.

In the historic region of what is now the nation of Turkey, where some of the first New Testament churches were established and flourished, the TBN affiliate network Kanal Hayat is reaching millions of Turkish-speaking individuals with the message of God's love.

The partnership with TBN first began in 2014 when Matt and Laurie Crouch traveled to Turkey to meet with Christian leaders who had launched Kanal Hayat to share God's love with the largely Muslim population in the region.

As Matt and Laurie spoke with the leadership they discovered that thousands were coming to Christ through the network. Since 2016, when Kanal Hayat officially joined the TBN family of networks, those numbers have steadily increased.

Today through its online presence Kanal Hayat reaches Turkish-speaking viewers across the earth with the hope and grace only Jesus can give.

A Miracle of Peace in the Middle East

On September 15, 2020, President Donald Trump, Israeli Prime Minister Benjamin Netanyahu, and representatives from Bahrain and the United Arab Emirates met at the White House to sign the groundbreaking Middle East peace agreement known as the Abraham Accords. Guided largely by the Trump administration, the agreement paved the way for the normalization of diplomatic relations between Israel and a core of Middle East nations.

TBN's documentary series *The Abraham Accords*, hosted by former U.S. Ambassador to Israel David Friedman, explores the complex process that guided the agreement. Filmed around the world, *The Abraham Accords* features interviews with former President Trump, former Vice President Mike Pence, former Secretary of State Mike Pompeo, Prime Minister Benjamin Netanyahu, and other leaders and experts.

Said Matt Crouch: "The Abraham Accords will undoubtedly go down in history as one of the most significant measures ever taken to encourage peace in the Middle East."

> "The sons of Abraham are back together for the first time in 3,000 years."
>
> — David Friedman, former U.S. Ambassador to Israel, producer, *The Abraham Accords*

EPISODE ONE: Descendants of Abraham

EPISODE TWO: Light at the End of the Tunnel

EPISODE THREE: Legacy of Blessing

EPISODE FOUR: People to People

President Trump with leaders of the nations signing the Abraham Accords peace initiative.

Former U.S. Ambassador to the United Nations Nikki Haley (left) and Matt Crouch with former U.S. Ambassador to Israel David Friedman.

ROUTE 60
THE BIBLICAL HIGHWAY

AMBASSADOR
DAVID FRIEDMAN

SECRETARY
MIKE POMPEO

FOLLOW AN ANCIENT ROAD
TO A BRIGHTER FUTURE
IN THEATERS STARTING SEPTEMBER 18th
Route60.movie

Hosts David Friedman and Mike Pompeo pause at a historic biblical site.

Route 60: The Biblical Highway represents the commitment TBN has to tell the fascinating story of the nation of Israel and its importance—past, present, and future—to our world. "

— Matt Crouch

Running from Nazareth in the north to Beersheba roughly 100 miles south, Israel's famed Route 60 is one of the world's most historic highways, traversing the landscape where much of Scripture actually occurred.

In May 2020 former U.S. Ambassador to Israel David Friedman and former U.S. Secretary of State Mike Pompeo took to the ancient road to film the TBN theatrical release *Route 60: The Biblical Highway*. Traveling major sections of the highway, often referred to as "The Way of the Patriarchs," the two seasoned diplomats discussed the historical significance of Route 60 and what it represents to our world today.

Friedman told the *Jerusalem Post* that the goal of the film is both to inform and challenge viewers about the relevance of Scripture to our present world. "At every stop we explain what happened," he said, "anything from Jesus' birth to the burial of Rachel along the side of the road." He added: "I want people to understand that many of the values we hold dear today come from the Bible and these places."

Sitting down with David Friedman and Mike Pompeo in Jerusalem.

Sending the Hope and Grace of Jesus to the World | TBN50

Centerpoint: *Current Events From a Christian Worldview*

More than ever followers of Jesus need a reliable mooring of truth in a sea of rapidly changing ideas that conflict with their faith. TBN's *Centerpoint*, a nightly program of current events and biblical perspective, was created to fill that void. *Centerpoint* addresses events and issues across our world, clarifying complex viewpoints, delivering truth with balance, and turning information into tools Christians can use every day.

With a guest lineup of professionals, experts, and respected Christian leaders, *Centerpoint* has become a nightly destination for faith-minded viewers who value accurate information from a Christian worldview.

STATE OF US ECONOMY

SATISFIED

DISSATISFIED

Behind the scenes.

> **"M**y decades in network television news have demonstrated that whichever channel delivers truth in an interesting way eventually garners the most viewers. And the best-informed viewers live the most meaningful lives.**"**
>
> — Michael Clemente, *Centerpoint* Senior Producer

Eye on Israel and the Middle East

Throughout its history TBN has been at the forefront of encouraging Christians to support the nation of Israel. That's why we've put so much energy into creating programming to inform and encourage our viewers about Israel and its important role in the Middle East — and the world. With powerful information and perspective, TBN viewers take an active role in praying for and blessing this nation and people so dear to God's heart.

While TBN has produced many unforgettable series and specials focused on Israel and the Middle East, here are three of our most informative and inspiring.

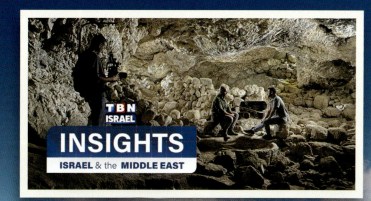

Insights: Israel & the Middle East. Hosted by TBN Israel's Samuel Smadja and Mati Shoshani, *Insights Israel* offers an inside view of modern Israel, featuring reports about innovations by the nation and people, along with faith stories about Israelis who are making a difference.

The Watchman With Erick Stakelbeck explores current events in the Middle East and how they impact Israel, America, and the world.

The Rosenberg Report. Filmed in Jerusalem and hosted by *New York Times* bestselling author Joel C. Rosenberg, each week *The Rosenberg Report* brings viewers insights and biblical perspective on important current events and issues across Israel and the Middle East.

> **"We are blessed to produce so much great content that communicates the truth about the miracle of Israel to viewers across the earth."**
>
> **— Samuel Smadja, TBN Israel**

Bright City Music leads in worship for a live TBN UK Praise program.

Pastor and author Ben Lindsay speaks about crime and violence among UK youth.

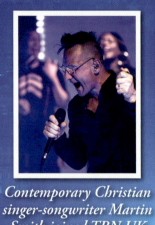

Archbishop of Canterbury Justin Welby appeared on TBN UK to speak about restorative justice.

Contemporary Christian singer-songwriter Martin Smith joined TBN UK for a behind-the-scenes worship concert.

Pastor and speaker Dr. R.T. Kendall has been one of TBN UK's popular ministry voices.

Mustard Seed Faith

"I can still remember the moment like it just happened. My father, Paul Crouch, and I were in a car with our TBN Europe representative, Richard Fleming, traveling through the English countryside, discussing the major financial step of faith it would take to launch TBN UK. Richard had explained that TBN's presence across the UK would cost nearly $1 million per month, a figure that caused my father to pause. "Wow! That's a lot of money," he exclaimed quietly, thinking about the countless individuals who partnered with TBN each month with their hard-earned dollars and heartfelt prayers.

In the middle of our conversation however, my dad, who had been gazing out the window for some time, suddenly asked:

"What are these fields of yellow crops we've been passing?" While Richard and I had been oblivious to the surrounding countryside, my dad, always a Missouri farm boy at heart, had caught sight of field after vast field of a bright yellow crop in bloom, and he was now insistent on knowing what it was these English farmers were growing. As we drove along, mulling over the pros, cons, risks, and rewards of a TBN network blanketing the UK, my father continued to be uncharacteristically distracted by these mysterious fields of brilliant yellow.

Suddenly our stoic Arab driver turned in his seat and uttered one emphatic word that answered the mystery of the fields of yellow, and seemed to give my dad confirmation about his decision: "Mustard!"

That one word was like a prophetic message from God, reminding my dad of Jesus' admonition that if we have faith the size of a tiny mustard seed, we could move any mountain that stood in our way. Yes, a million dollars a month seemed like a huge obstacle, but with even a little faith in God that million-dollar mountain could be pushed aside and tens of millions of individuals and families would have the life-changing message of Jesus available to them right in their homes."

— Matt Crouch

TBN | UK Hope for Britain

Mega Mix *is just one of the many entertaining and engaging programs for children airing on TBN UK.*

Host Emily Martin welcomes UK Pastor William McDowell on the TBN Meets *program.*

The London Community Gospel Choir performed for a special TBN UK Christmas program.

Each year TBN UK provides extensive coverage of the Big Church Festival, Europe's largest Christian music event.

Christian philanthropist Ken Costa hosted a TBN UK Easter special.

J anuary 5, 2015, marked one of the most significant moments in the history of Christian television with the launch of TBN UK on Freeview, the United Kingdom's free-to-air digital service that reaches 95 percent of every television household across England, Scotland, Wales, and Northern Ireland. Today through Freeview, the UK-wide Sky broadcast platform, and TBN UK's online app, over 65 million individuals across the British Isles can now receive a broad range of faith-and-family programming 24 hours a day.

Matt recalled that the first movements toward the launch of TBN UK began in 2013, shortly before the passing of his father, TBN founder Paul Crouch Sr., who personally signed the initiative to establish the Christian network. "As a pioneer in faith broadcasting my father was responsible for taking Christian television to hundreds of millions of people on every inhabited continent," said Matt. "But the launch of TBN UK represents one of the largest single increases of Christian television coverage in history, giving nearly every household in the United Kingdom access to life-transforming Christian television. In the years since the launch of TBN UK we still marvel at how God made it all happen."

Of course, it's no secret that Britain has a rich, centuries-long heritage of sharing the Christian faith with the rest of the world. "America, for one, owes its own tradition of faith in God in large part to the men and women who came from Britain to preach and teach the gospel," said Matt. "And TBN is humbled to help give back to this nation and people through the ministry of TBN UK. Our prayer is that this broadcast outreach will continue to have a huge impact across the United Kingdom and beyond in the decades ahead."

Find out more about TBN's outreach across the United Kingdom and experience it for yourself online at **TBN.uk**.

> "... the addition of TBN UK represents one of the largest single increases of Christian television coverage in history...."
> – Matt Crouch

TBN Africa and TBN Yetu are reaching millions across the continent with the love of Jesus.

Celebrating a TBN Africa milestone.

Angus Buchan, author of Faith Like Potatoes.

Through its state-of-the-art production studio in Johannesburg, TBN Africa is reaching the entire African continent and beyond with dynamic, life-changing programming.

TBN Africa: Covering a Continent

TBN Africa director Lucky Mbiko and Doreen King host the network's Partner Time program.

Lucky Mbiko with former South African Chief Justice Mogoeng.

Singer Lebohang Kgapola on TBN Africa.

TBN's rich history in Africa reaches all the way back to the 1980s, when Lennox Sebe, the president of South Africa's Ciskei homeland, invited TBN founder Paul Crouch to establish a station in his country. "President Sebe gave us the permit to build our first station in Ciskei," recalled Paul, "and with that a door was opened for the birth of TBN on Africa's southern tip."

The launch of that first station paved the way for stations in the Transkei and Bophuthatswana homelands, and, ultimately, to an entire network called TBN Africa, that today covers the entirety of sub-Saharan Africa — and beyond — with life-changing programming, much of it from pastors, Christian leaders, and ministries on the ground across the African continent.

And with a new, state-of-the art production studio in Johannesburg, along with the addition of a second exciting Africa lifestyle network, TBN Yetu, TBN is poised to reach new generations of African viewers with a broad range of faith-and-family programming that is authentic, Afro-centric, and thought-provoking.

"We are excited for all the incredible doors God is opening for us to reach people, families, and communities across Africa," said Lucky Mbiko, director of TBN Africa. "These are exciting and fruitful days as TBN spreads the love of Jesus to all Africans."

> "These are exciting and fruitful days as TBN spreads the love of Jesus to all Africans."
>
> – Lucky Mbiko

Added Matt Crouch: "Over forty years ago my father came to Africa with a sense of faith and expectancy, as TBN first went on the air in Ciskei. Today that bold move of faith and obedience to God's call continues to reap a harvest of souls as TBN Africa faithfully delivers the good news of God's love to hundreds of millions of individuals and families across the African continent and beyond."

*Find out more about TBN's broadcast outreach across the continent of Africa, and view it for yourself, at **TBNAfrica.org** and **TBNYetu.org**.*

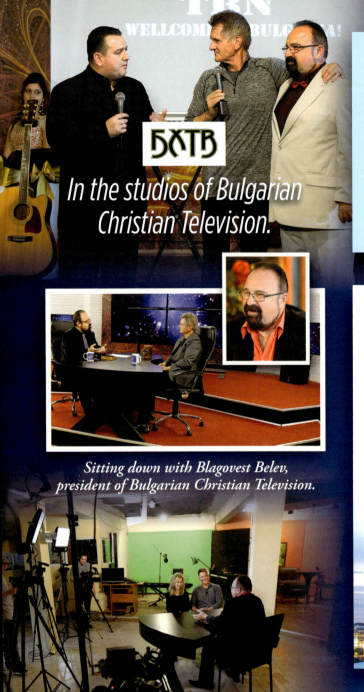

In the studios of Bulgarian Christian Television.

Sitting down with Blagovest Belev, president of Bulgarian Christian Television.

TBN Francophone is reaching France with round-the-clock life-changing digital content.

TBNFR

Télévison Bonne Nouvelle

In the years since its launch TBN Francophone has become the second largest and most popular evangelical Christian media network for the French-speaking world.

SOYEZ FIDÈLE À VOTRE APPELLE

Reaching Sweden and Northern Europe with the love of Jesus

TBN NORDIC

TBN Nordic is touching a potential audience of tens of millions of viewers with life-changing Christian programming.

TBN UA

God's Hope and Grace to the Nations

While TBN has spared no effort throughout our history to reach entire continents with life-changing networks, God has also given us the opportunity to target specific people groups.

That includes Bulgaria, which suffered decades of oppression under communist rule. But there has been a deep hunger for God across Bulgaria, and in 2015 TBN partnered with a local pastor to launch Bulgarian Christian Television (BCT). Today BCT reaches more than 85 percent of Bulgarian households with life-changing programming.

TBN is also impacting viewers across Sweden and Scandinavia through TBN Nordic, which began as an effort by Swedish businessman Anders Wisth to reach Sweden's largely secular audience with the love of Jesus. Since 2018 TBN Nordic has been reaching viewers in Sweden, Norway, Denmark, Finland, and other northern European countries with God's love.

Across the earth, millions of French-speaking viewers are being impacted through the digital TBN Francophone network. Using the power of YouTube and Facebook, the online TBN network is reaching throughout France, Europe, Africa, Canada, and beyond with compelling content designed to entertain and inspire, while clearly communicating a message of hope and salvation through Jesus.

And in 2022, as the lives of millions of Ukrainian individuals and families were torn apart by the violence of war, TBN launched TBN UA, a dedicated digital network focused on reaching Ukrainian people with the message of Jesus. Through this 24-hour viewing platform Ukrainians can experience the peace and assurance of the gospel any time and anywhere in their own language.

Revelation 7:9 gives us a breathtaking description of a vast numbers of individuals at the end of the age worshipping before God's throne — "a great multitude which no one could number, of all nations, tribes, peoples, and tongues...." Said Matt Crouch: "This is our heart at TBN, to reach every nation and people with the message of God's love."

> "This is our heart at TBN, to reach every nation and people with the message of God's love."
> – Matt Crouch

Early in the war with Russia TBN UA's production team was on the ground daily taping programming to provide encouragement and hope to Ukrainian families in crisis.

Led by Vitaly Stebenev, TBN UA is helping meet both the physical and spiritual needs of individuals and families in Ukraine with a demonstration of God's love in action.

TBN2ND CHANCE™
Restoring Hope to Inmates

"Jesus is clear that when we reach out with hope and healing to these incarcerated men and women, we are touching His heart of compassion."

— C.J. Orndorff
TBN 2nd Chance

Visiting with Burl Cain, an expert on reforming prisons and inmates from the inside out.

TBN 2nd Chance: Light in the Darkness

Nearly two million men and women are serving time in America's prisons — and TBN wants to take God's hope and healing to each of them! That's why we launched TBN 2nd Chance back in 2007, and in the years since then countless individuals serving time in prisons have been impacted by the outreach. Today TBN 2nd Chance is providing 24-hour life-changing Christian television to more than one million adults and juveniles serving time in over 800 prisons across 41 states.

At every prison, TBN 2nd Chance pays the cost of equipment and installation, providing inmates with networks like our **TBN** flagship network, along with **TBN Inspire**, our **Positiv** channel, featuring wholesome movies and entertainment, and **Enlace**, TBN's Spanish-language affiliate network.

And what's the result? An inmate in Mississippi wrote to tell us: "I am in my seventh year of a life sentence without parole. I recently started watching TBN, and I came to know Christ here in prison.... Thank you for being a light in this dark place." And a prisoner in Virginia wrote to say: "Thank you for all your efforts and support in helping us to change the course of our future with Christ Jesus in our lives."

C.J. Orndorff, musician and evangelist with TBN 2nd Chance, emphasized that for Christ followers, sharing Jesus with those who are in prison is not optional. "Whether you're personally going into prisons or helping others who do, Jesus is clear that when we reach out with hope and healing to these incarcerated men and women, we are touching His heart of compassion," he explained. "Jesus expects us to take salvation, hope, healing, and encouragement wherever there's a need — including prisons."

The TBN 2nd Chance team often visits prisons to share God's love with inmates face-to-face. Director Mark Reynolds said that such meetings bring a personal element to the outreach: "When inmates look us in the eye and say how the daily presence of TBN programming brings hope to their lives — nothing can top that."

> "Thank you for being a light in this dark place."
> – Mississippi Inmate

FRIENDS OF TBN

TBN's flagship ministry, music, and talk show *Praise* features a wide range of inspiring guests from across the Christian community, from pastors and Christian leaders, to popular and influential authors, musicians, celebrities, statesmen, and more.

Chris Tomlin *Gary Chapman* *Andy Stanley* *Charles Stanley* *Bobby Schuller* *Christine and Nick Caine* *Andrea Bocelli*

 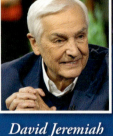  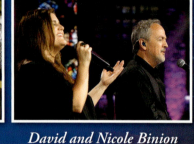   

Erwin McManus *David Jeremiah* *Sheila Walsh* *David and Nicole Binion* *Max Lucado* *Joyce Meyer* *Eric Metaxas*

Javen Campbell *James Brown and Tony Dungy* *John Hagee* *Mike Rowe* *Matt and Laurie with Prince Ermias Selassie*

Grammy-winning Christian singer-songwriter Michael W. Smith has hosted multiple TBN worship specials.

Enjoying a moment with gospel music legends Bill and Gloria Gaither.

Greg Laurie *Franklin Graham* *Donald Trump* *Benjamin Netanyahu* *Jentezen Franklin* *Joel Rosenberg* *Erick Stakelbeck*

David Green

Jekalyn Carr

John Bevere

Pastor Mark Batterson

Steven Furtick

T.D. Jakes

Louie Giglio

Joel and Victoria Osteen

Jason Crabb

Brian 'Head' Welch

Jason Sobel

Samuel Rodriguez

Robert Jeffress

Kirk Cameron

Robert Morris

Jordan Rubin and Josh Axe

Shawn Bolz

Scott Hannen

Lisa Harper

Kathie Lee Gifford

Blynda Lane

Dave Stotts

Dennis Haysbert

TBN host Blynda Lane (right) interviews gospel music legend CeCe Winans.

Shannon Bream

Les and Leslie Parrott

David Friedman

Mike Pompeo

O.S. Hawkins

Rick Warren

Mike Huckabee

Tyler Perry

Joseph Prince

Tom Newman hosted the producers of The Chosen series, which aired on TBN.

"If you wind the clock back fifty years from where we're standing today, you'd see my dad ordering steel, concrete, and building materials to build towers, antennas, and the distribution system for television around the world. Today we're still building, but those materials are going for studios and sound stages that will create a non-stop supply of life-changing content to fill a global distribution system my parents would never even have dreamed of in their day."

— Matt and Laurie Crouch

UNDER CONSTRUCTION: *New production facility in Dallas, Texas.*

Reaching the Next Generation

TBN is committed to reaching every age group with God's love.

Fifty years after its miraculous launch in 1973, TBN has grown into a family of networks reaching every corner of the earth with the gospel message. By far the most miraculous part of those fifty years has been the more than forty million men, women, and children who have come to faith in Christ because of TBN's global outreach.

But there's a growing generation across the earth who desperately needs the hope and healing that only Jesus can bring. In fact, noted Matt Crouch, over half the world's population of nearly eight billion people are under the age of thirty. "Here at TBN we carry a special burden for this generation of individuals and families who live in a very different world than many of us grew up in," he said. "The temptations, dangers, and confusion they face are far greater than existed even a few short years ago. More than ever the world needs a clarion voice declaring that Jesus is truth and life in a broken and chaotic world."

Sadly, the deteriorating state of our world, where opposition to the gospel of Jesus Christ seems to be growing by the day, has caused many Christians to grow passive and pessimistic.

"But now is not the time to be silenced," challenged Matt. "God is still calling His people to engage in the great global harvest of souls through prayer, partnering with ministries like TBN, and by reaching out to our neighbors and the nations."

Jesus declared that the gospel must be preached "in all the world as a witness to all the nations, and then the end will come" (Matthew 24:14). Said Matt: "It's clear that the end hasn't come yet. There's still time for each of us to say 'yes' to God's call to help others find peace through Christ. It's the most important and far-reaching thing you'll ever do in this life. Will you join our TBN family in reaching this generation with the love of Jesus?"

> "More than ever we need a clarion voice declaring that Jesus is truth and life in a broken and chaotic world."
> — Matt Crouch